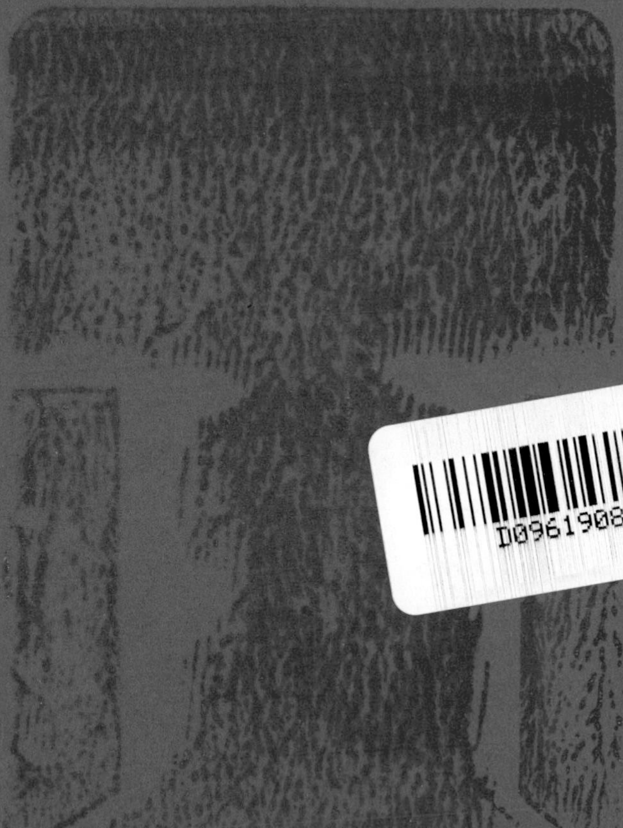

PACIFIC ISLANDS LITERATURE

Pacific Islands Literature

ONE HUNDRED BASIC BOOKS

A. GROVE DAY

THE UNIVERSITY PRESS OF HAWAII
HONOLULU 1971

Library of Congress Catalog Card Number 70-151452
Published by The University Press of Hawaii
(formerly University of Hawaii Press, ISBN 0-87022-180-9)

Printed in the United States of America

Photograph on page 72 courtesy of Honolulu Academy of Arts

To the
Best Agents in the World,
PAUL R. REYNOLDS
and
OLIVER G. SWAN

Contents

Preface

GOOD READING ABOUT THE SOUTH SEAS

Once James A. Michener and I devised a quiz that would enable us to judge the validity of anyone's claim to be an Old Pacific Hand. We decided that, in addition to having traveled somewhat among the islands, he should be well grounded in the classic books about the South Seas—in other words, should have a knowledge, at least in English, of Pacific literature. Nothing less would satisfy us.

Pacific literature—what is that? It embodies the best writings about the Pacific Ocean region, the books that evoke the flavor and fascination of the real South Seas. Until now, the great need for an introduction to this branch of literature in English has not been met.

Selectivity is required. Writings about the Pacific region form a tidal wave of print. For instance, the second edition of Professor C. R. H. Taylor's *A Pacific Bibliography* (1965) confines itself to works relating to the native peoples of Oceania; it runs to some fifteen thousand titles previous to 1960, and merely lists writing of ethnological rather than literary interest—only two books by Robert Louis Stevenson are mentioned. *Bibliotheca Polynesiana*, a 1969 catalog of the Bjarne Kroepelein collection in Oslo, gives 1,368 titles, and omits some items not easily attainable. *A Bibliography of Bibliographies of the South Pacific*, by Ida Emily Leeson, needs much updating since 1954. How is one to find his way to the best literary works among the towering shelves of the Pacific collections of the world?

A selective, annotated guide through this mass of literary material is herein supplied in the hope of aiding the student, the teacher, the collector, the librarian, and—most of all—the informed reader who enjoys losing himself on a ship, or among exotic islands, or on high Pacific peaks, or in cannibal villages of the jungle, or among the Polynesian belles of a Tahitian streamside.

The Pacific is the world's most romantic ocean, the most remote from mankind's cities, and it was the last to be explored. The rediscovery of its islands in the sixteenth century was almost an accident in the broad attempt by Europeans to open a new route to the Spice Islands of the East Indies, as well as to discover an imagined southern continent that they persisted in inserting on the map with the label *Terra Australis Incognita*. The mixing of European and "native" blood in the islands of this largest of oceans began in 1521, when the crew of the *Vittoria*, one of Ferdinand Magellan's ships on the first voyage around the world, landed in Micronesia. But the South Seas had been discovered and named by Vasco Nuñez de Balboa in 1512. For Balboa, at Panama, the ocean did indeed lie to the south, and he claimed for Spain everything that lay inside its basin or bordered its yet unknown shores.

The discovery of the Pacific in fiction came more than two centuries after Balboa. Daniel Defoe's early, most famous novel, *The Life and Strange Surprizing Adventures of Robinson Crusoe* (1719), which set the pattern for desert-island tales, was based on the true story of Alexander Selkirk's survival on an island of the Juan Fernández group in the South Pacific. Defoe, however, shifted the setting to the Caribbean. Public lack of geographical knowledge enabled Defoe, astonishingly, in 1725 also to sell as factual a volume called *A New Voyage Round the World by a Course Never Sailed Before*, purely a work of his imagination. No one at the time could call him a liar.

The Pacific was almost the last place left on earth where a writer could set a story in which almost anything was likely to happen. When Jonathan Swift, in 1726, published that great book usually called *Gulliver's Travels*, the accompanying maps showed that all his imaginary lands lay in unexplored regions of the Pacific. Lilliput was northwest of Van Diemen's Land (Tasmania). Brobdingnag was a peninsula in the ocean north of the "New Albion" (now called California) of Francis Drake. The islands in Part III were east of Japan, and the isle of the Houyhyhnms, the noble horses, was south of "New Holland", or Australia.

The rise of Romanticism in the eighteenth century brought a number of new strains to literature. One of the foremost was nostalgia for the primitive. It is no accident that accounts of voyages and travels were high among the favorite reading of the time. Many people sought to find in such books a place where imagination could have full play, undisturbed by the nasty facts that realists delighted to unearth. Another strong tenet of Romanticism was: "If you can't find the reality of your dream, invent it." Horace Walpole erected a ruined abbey on his estate and even paid a hermit to haunt it. The need was great among such dreamers to find a heaven on earth.

Jean-Jacques Rousseau can be praised or blamed for seeking the Golden Age among savages. In 1749 the Academy of Dijon offered a prize for an essay on the effect of the progress of civilization on morals. Sentimental and perverse, Rousseau took the negative side and tried to show that primitive societies were, paradoxically, more moral and happy. Primitive men, he argued, were on the whole freer than any others, because the equality intended by God was spoiled by social organization. The greatest advantage of primitive life, though, was that the physical and moral aspects of sex were not at war, so that neither love nor jealousy troubled the innocent pagan. Speaking of Rousseau's idea, one writer said: "It was hardly worth while for natural men to fight each other over natural women."

Rousseau's discourse, which appeared in 1750, won the prize and brought him admiring readers. The Noble Savage became all the rage. Since few uncorrupted savages could be found in the Old World, the hopes of the Romantics lay in the New World. For a while the American Indians were the ideal. But the more the civilized world found out about the Indians of the Americas, the less possible it was to believe in their romantic nobility. The last remaining region where primitive people, unspoiled by civilization, might be found was the South Seas.

The voyagers did their best to find noble savages there. More than two centuries ago, on June 18, 1767, Samuel Wallis and the crew of the British round-the-world ship *Dolphin* discovered the green-shrouded peaks of Tahiti. Their reception, after an initial attack by two thousand warriors in canoes, was warm. The buxom "Queen Oberea" befriended the captain and wept when he departed, after more than a month's refreshment on the island that was to become the most famous in the South Pacific.

The young ladies of Tahiti were charming, and at first their favors could be obtained for a tenpenny nail. Inflation soon set in, however, and finally the amorous sailors were trading their hammock spikes and even cleats torn from the *Dolphin's* deck. When Wallis found out about this, he "no longer wondered that the ship was in danger of being pulled to pieces for the nails and iron that held her together".

The gracious French explorer Louis Antoine de Bougainville arrived at Tahiti eight months later, and the account of his reception gave the strongest hope yet to seekers of free love and free coconuts. When the nymphs of the isle swam out to greet his ships, *Boudeuse* and *Etoile*, Bougainville christened the island "the New Cytherea", after the place where Aphrodite rose from the waves.

Captain James Cook first arrived in the South Seas in 1769. His chastity was notorious among both his shipmates and the island peoples, and he was shocked by some of the primitive customs. But Cook's rewrite man, Dr. John Hawkesworth, in his *Voyages* (1773), knew well how to play up the spicy bits. From then on, even in England, the Polynesian became a full-fledged member of the roster of Noble Savages. The visits to London of such well-mannered South Sea Islanders as Omai of Huahine and Prince Lee Boo of the Palau group did nothing to harm the image of primitive charmers. The two young men were lionized by British society.

Thus the questing romanticists found in the Pacific what they were determined to find. But there was another side to the picture that emerged. There were also the realists, not content to dwell in dreams when a hemisphere was attainable for examination at first hand—a hemisphere to be charted, to be studied scientifically, peopled by unusual human beings of many sorts who might be converted, enslaved, or imitated. The literature of the South Seas began to include latitudes and lunar sights, shark bites and spear wounds, scurvy, wrecks on saw-edged reefs, hurricanes, and the ovens of the man-eaters. Fortunately, among the realists as among the romanticizers, there were men able to record the Pacific world for our delight today. When Magellan the Circumnavigator first crossed its rolling solitudes in 1521 and there met his death, his journalizing friend Pigafetta was at hand to relate the episode. Afterwards came other articulate mariners—Dampier and Cook and Bligh and La Pérouse, and a fleet of other names—and their tales of mutiny and shipwreck, and battles with brown natives, still live for us in their lines of print.

The canvas becomes more crowded, and the writers are missionaries, pearl hunters, Polynesian preachers, convicts, beachcombers, supercargoes, deserters from the brutalities of a clipper's surging deck, scientists such as Darwin and Huxley, sun-hungry painters like La Farge and Gauguin, escapists from crowded old cities, and anthropologists and folklore collectors to unlock the mysteries of mores and myth. Here, in the tracks of the star-following navigators of outrigger canoes with matting sails, voyage the seamen of the Manila galleons and the mutineers of the *Bounty*. Here come the fiction writers, thrilling us as always with yarns of burning ships, open boats under a sizzling sun, the hearts of white men and brown women, the remittance man, the wreckers, the imp in the devil's bottle. Here are poets like Rupert Brooke and Robert D. FitzGerald. Here are men of letters known the world over—Herman Melville and "Pierre Loti" and Robert Louis Stevenson and Jack London and Somerset Maugham. Here is good reading in God's plenty.

There are several themes that run through Pacific literature which, aside from similarities of locale, unify this genre. "The essential elements of typical South Sea stories," says one early anthologist, "appear to be, first, the region (with uncertain boundaries); second, adventure of one kind or another; third, freedom from conventionality, or an unusualness according to present-day 'civilized' ideas. Undoubtedly this freedom from formality constitutes much of the glamor of the South Seas, and in it lies the real charm of South Sea literature" (E. C. Parnwell, *Stories of the South Seas*, 1928).

One immediate problem is to define the locale. The boundaries of the Pacific region differ according to the purposes of the geographer, the scientist, the anthropologist. For the student of literature, it seems desirable to limit the area to Oceania—that is, the islands of Micronesia, Melanesia, and Polynesia. One does not thereby imply that Japan and Indonesia and Chile are not Pacific regions, nor for that matter California or Alaska. There is enough, however, to occupy us with the best books that have dealt with Oceania. Books primarily about Hawaii and New Zealand, although these groups of islands fall properly within the Polynesian Triangle, have not here been reviewed; they will be dealt with in two other volumes planned for the present series.

All the authors included in my selected list have at least visited the Pacific, and many of them have dwelt there for many years. Omissions from this list have been made with a heavy hand. One apparent omission is a book by Joseph Conrad. Somehow the idea has sprung up that Conrad wrote a great deal about the Pacific islands. Actually he set many tales on the China coast or in Southeast Asia or the Philippines. Only one short story was set in Oceania—"The Planter of Malata", about a Melanesian isle.

The voyage of Richard Henry Dana, described in *Two Years Before the Mast* (1840), touched only at one Pacific island, Juan Fernández; Dana does, however, describe some "Sandwich-Islanders" he met in California. In any case, Dana's book is well enough known to require no commendation here.

Scores of books have been done by yachtsmen who ran through the South Seas and made snapshots of Papeete or Pago Pago: few of these have lasting merit. Nor have the profound observations of globetrotters who stayed on an island between ships and became instant experts. Omitted also are a number of undoubtedly entertaining writers of South Sea fiction, such as Beatrice Grimshaw, A. Saffroni-Middleton, John Russell, E. L. Grant-Watson, Ralph Stock, Russell Foreman, Olaf Ruhen, Robert Keable, Geoffrey Cotterell, and "James Meade" (James Arthur Stewart). After World War I the spate of "through-the-South-Seas-with-rod-and-camera" books earned a deserved parody in *The Cruise of the "Kawa"* (1921) by "Dr. Walter E. Traprock". A jumble of "desert island stuff" turned out for the magazine market has been discarded from consideration. Most of such books were manufactured by city dwellers who never went to the Pacific. R. M. Ballantyne, for example, gave up writing about the South Seas because he stated through ignorance that coconuts grew without husks, and made similar gross errors. Books for children are also omitted, along with detective novels and ephemeral thrillers.

World War II in the Pacific produced surprisingly few important novels, aside from James A. Michener's *Tales of the South Pacific* and Ira Wolfert's *An Act of Love*. The American Army might not be proud of James Jones's *From Here to Eternity*, and the American Navy might wish that Herman Wouk's *The "Caine" Mutiny* had not been published. Those who would praise Norman Mailer's *The Naked and the Dead* might be disillusioned on rereading it. Mailer's war is limited to a small group of men on a small, imaginary island, and the most deadly warfare takes place within the American ranks. The book is inflated by Mailer's digressions and repetitive biographies, and few views of native people or South Pacific settings are given. The most disappointing aspect of *The Naked and the Dead*, however, is its use of a war setting to show a far different kind of fight—the class struggle. Mailer's novel is in essence a Marxist allegory.

Fiction about imaginary Pacific islands has appeared ever since the days of Swift and Defoe, but will be merely mentioned here. The earliest American example to be found is by the Midwestern author Timothy Flint. Most of the action of his *Life and Adventures of Arthur Clenning* (1828) takes place on an unpeopled South Sea island, and its main source was *Robinson Crusoe*. Shipwrecked, Arthur rescues haughty Augusta Wellman, and they and their baby start a new society. The tone is highly moral. Edgar Allan Poe capitalized on popular interest in *The Narrative of Arthur Gordon Pym of Nantucket* (1838), which deals in Poesque style with mutiny, shipwreck, and horrible sufferings in the South Seas. It was based on Benjamin Morrell's *Narrative of Four Voyages to the South Seas and Pacific* (1832) and a proposed expedition by J. N. Reynolds. James Fenimore Cooper's *The Crater, or Vulcan's Peak* (1847) presents his idea of Utopia in the form of an ideal colony of select people in a volcanic archipelago. He may have been inspired by the success of Herman Melville's novels *Typee* (1846) and *Omoo* (1847). Melville himself, in 1849, used an invented archipelago to provide a multiplicity of settings in *Mardi*. Each island offered a different set of customs and a different challenge to the questing narrator, Taji. American books of our century include *October Island* (1952) by "William March" and *Islandia* (1942), a gigantic creation by an American law professor, rewritten from his notes by his wife and daughter ten years after his death.

British writers have been especially fond of setting stories on imaginary South Sea islands. Any list would have to include H. de Vere Stacpoole's *The Blue Lagoon: A Romance* (1908); Rose Macaulay's *Orphan Island* (1924); Archibald Marshall's *That Island* (1927); and Sylvia Townsend Warner's *Mr. Fortune's Maggot* (1927). Among the best is J. B. Priestley's *Faraway* (1932). Much later, Jacquetta Hawkes, who had become Mrs. Priestley, wrote *Providence Island* (1959), about a group of archeologists who find in Melanesia the remnant of the Magdalenian people. William Golding's *Lord of the Flies* (1954) chose a Pacific island on which to dump a plane load of boys, aged six to twelve; there, during a nuclear war of the future, they could form tribal gangs, harry the heroic and the poetic lads, and regress to the worship of Beelzebub. Aldous Huxley's last novel, *Island* (1962), portrays a brave new island world. Corruption enters in the shape of a shifty journalist, and the noble, primitive people become subjects of a self-appointed raja.

Herein I have selected one hundred books, from the many about the real Pacific, to review at more or less length. I have not attempted to set up an official canon to limit the pleasures of discovery, but have merely tried to demonstrate the richness of the literary offerings in English from the Pacific region. It is quite possible that some of the titles in the appendix, "Some Additional References on the Pacific Islands", should have been included among the hundred, and others demoted. I hope I have not overlooked anyone's favorite classic. I have not defined "literature" for my purpose so rigidly as to leave out any really good volume. Although all the books deal with one broad setting, my test is whether the book chosen would be read for its charm or power, regardless of setting.

My purpose, then, is to share with other readers some products of thirty years of seeking, in libraries from London to Sydney, books about the Pacific that have literary qualities, and to make known some of my reasons for choosing them above others. To collect samples of writings by many authors, I have published nine volumes of anthologies of Pacific literature in English, five of them in collaboration with Professor Carl Stroven. My debt to my colleague Dr. Stroven, who spent forty years reading in this area and pioneering in searching out works of quality, is here acknowledged once more. It was he who originated in 1936 the lecture course at the University of Hawaii entitled "Literature of the Pacific"—a unique course which I had the pleasure of offering for a decade and which is still given by others at Honolulu. My service at this University during a quarter of a century, with its opportunities for discussion with people from many Pacific countries, as well as my travels in the South Seas, have furthered my interest in combining leisure reading and criticism. Special thanks for splendid co-operation go to the staffs of the Hawaiian and Pacific Collection at the University of Hawaii, the Hawaii State Library, the Mitchell and Dixson Libraries in Sydney, and the National Library at Canberra, Australia.

Users of *Pacific Islands Literature: 100 Basic Books* should be aware of some of the methods followed. The reviews actually deal with one hundred authors, although the most outstanding work of each is the primary topic. Information is given about other writings by these authors on the Pacific islands, and some biographical information that might be pertinent. Books by other writers on similar subjects are sometimes mentioned. The arrangement by number is chronological, based on the date of the first episode in any series of events. The first items cover prehistory, folklore, and general works; then with Pigafetta begins the Magellan story, which is followed by writings about other voyages and adventures, and so on to more recent times. Reading these reviews in this order might serve as a rough outline of Pacific history as well as Pacific literature. The length of a review is not necessarily an indication of importance. The title numbers are used for cross-references in the reviews; the discussion of Bligh's book (No. 27) naturally calls for a request to see the review of *The "Bounty" Trilogy* by Nordhoff and Hall (No. 29). The Index of Names and Places in the appendix may be used not only to locate mentions of main authors but to show what has been written on various islands or groups. Only books in English are reviewed, but some of these, of course, are translations. (A similar outline on French literature about the Pacific islands might well be written by someone better qualified.) Only first editions of books reviewed are given. An English edition precedes others, even though an American edition might have antedated it. The inclusion of names of publishers, although calling for much troublesome research, should be of value in tracing editions. Later editions, especially transitory paperbacks, are not usually mentioned. Spellings and other mechanics attempt to follow those given in *Webster's Third New International Unabridged Dictionary* (Springfield, Mass.: G. & C. Merriam, 1965). Geographical terms follow *Index to the Map of the Pacific Ocean* (Washington, D.C.: National Geographic Society, 1965). Bibliographic entries follow those recommended in *The MLA Style Sheet* (2nd. ed., New York: Modern Language Association of America, 1970). Titles of first editions (often shortened to save space) are, however, cited verbatim.

My choices have not been concerned with the present availability of copies. One additional value of this book, it is hoped, is that it might encourage the present tendency to reprint, perhaps with scholarly introductions, a number of fine volumes that have been lost in the deluge of later printed matter. Publishers are awakening to the demand for attractive and inexpensive editions of Pacific books.

If you have read most or all my hundred basic books—which would, I hope, form a good start toward a collection of Pacific island classics—you will certainly qualify for the honorable title of Old Pacific Hand!

A. Grove Day
Senior Professor of
English, Emeritus
University of Hawaii

There are few who do not retain the vivid recollections of their first perusal of Prince Leeboo, or Captain Cook's Voyages. Often, when a schoolboy, I have found the most gratifying recreation, for a winter's evening, in reading the account of the wreck of the *Antelope*, the discovery of Tahiti, and other narratives of a similar kind. Little, however, did I suppose, when in imagination I have followed the discoverer from island to island, and have gazed in fancy on their romantic hills and valleys, together with their strange but interesting inhabitants, that I should ever visit scenes, the description of which afforded me so much satisfaction.

WILLIAM ELLIS, *Polynesian Researches*, I

[1] WILLIAM WYATT GILL. *Myths and Songs from the South Pacific.* London: Henry S. King, 1876.

Most of the missionaries who went to Polynesia took little interest in the folk literature of the native people, regarding it as heathen lore that should be forgotten and supplanted by the stories of the Bible. The chief exception was W. W. Gill (1828–1896), who was born at Bristol, England, received the B.A. degree from the University of London, and was at the age of twenty-three chosen by the London Missionary Society as missionary to Mangaia, one of the Cook Islands. Stationed in this group for more than twenty years, deeply interested in the people, he learned their language thoroughly; and from converted native priests and chiefs he collected the traditional stories and poetry contained in his best known book, *Myths and Songs from the South Pacific*, published with an introduction by the philologist Friedrich Max Müller.

Gill's early collections were drawn upon by Katharine Luomala (see No. 7) and others for stories and songs, especially those concerning the demigod Maui.

[2] LORIMER FISON. *Tales from Old Fiji.* London: Alexander Moring, 1904.

Lorimer Fison (1832–1907), born at Barningham, Suffolk, left Cambridge University after his second term to seek gold in Australia. In Melbourne in 1863 he was ordained as a Methodist minister and was sent to Fiji, where he spent eight years as a missionary. From 1871 to 1875 Fison worked in New South Wales and Victoria, returning to Fiji from then until 1884 as head of an institution for training natives as teachers. He began publishing papers on anthropology, some of them in collaboration with Alfred William Howitt. In 1884 Fison returned to Australia, where he edited church publications and continued studies in anthropology until his death. *Tales from Old Fiji*, his only volume of popular interest, is narrated in entertaining style; some of the myths are presumably told by a Fijian informant, the old king of Lakemba.

[3] TEUIRA HENRY. *Ancient Tahiti.* Honolulu: Bishop Museum Bulletin No. 48, 1928.

Through the intelligent and devoted efforts of a granddaughter, the most valuable collection of literature on Tahitian culture was preserved.

The Rev. John Muggridge Orsmond (1784?–1856) was educated for the ministry at Gosport, England. When the opportunity came to engage in a mission to Tahiti, he accepted. He and his first wife, Mary, made a voyage on a convict ship to Sydney, during which they experienced a revolt by the prisoners, a fire aboard, and a brief pursuit by Algerian pirates. At Sydney they took a passage on the ship *Fox* for the Society group, reaching Mooréa in April 1817. Orsmond labored there, as well as at Huahine and Bora Bora, before settling at Tahiti in 1831. With driving energy the Englishman made the people of the islands accomplish material ends by building houses, churches, roads, and bridges. In his early years he even sacrificed for these ends the village breadfruit and coconut trees, feeling that a bountiful supply of food near at hand contributed to idleness.

On the ship from London, Orsmond had been lucky enough to find several Tahitians; he learned their language, and shortly after his arrival became fluent. He listened to chiefs, priests, landholders, and laborers, and from oral tradition recorded a wealth of facts and legends. The early Tahitian-English dictionary published by the London Missionary Society was mainly his work. Orsmond's manuscripts were heavily drawn upon by William Ellis (see No. 40). This bulky mass of documents, the result of thirty years of research, was delivered by Orsmond to the commandant of the protectorate as a gift to the people of France. The fate of the original manuscript is unknown; it was probably burned about 1850, during the Second Republic.

Teuira Henry (1847–1915) was born at Tahiti, granddaughter of

Orsmond and his second wife, Isabella; her father's parents were William Henry, missionary of the *Duff* (see No. 34), and his wife Sarah. The girl was educated at a mission school at Papeete, and thereafter taught French and English in the Viennot School for twenty years. A natural linguist, Miss Henry made a deep study of the old Tahitian tongue, much more archaic than the present dialect and resembling more closely the Hawaiian. She spent much of her time completing and correcting the papers left by Orsmond in her care. She moved to Hawaii and lived there from 1890 to 1905, teaching in the primary schools for more than a decade. She continued to work unceasingly on the manuscripts in Honolulu, where access to other Polynesian literature advanced her studies. She also contributed numerous papers to the *Journal of the Polynesian Society*. The last ten years of her life were spent in her native island.

Miss Henry's lifelong devotion to her task was rewarded posthumously when her heirs arranged that *Ancient Tahiti* should be painstakingly edited and published by the Bernice P. Bishop Museum. The volume, running to more than six hundred pages, contains many quotations in Tahitian and English in small type. Starting with accounts of the discovery of Tahiti and the visits of early explorers, the chapters cover the flora of the Society Islands, descriptions of the ancient land divisions, remarks on religion and the famed temple platforms, belief in magic and fire walking, social classes, royal genealogies, the life of the individual, warfare, and methods of reckoning. About half the book contains chants and legends. W. D. Alexander says in a preface: "There is a certain grandeur and poetry in some of these ancient chants, particularly in the account of the creation, which is not surpassed by that of any other primitive people." The style is clear and interesting, although not perhaps as sturdy as that of Miss Henry's grandfather in the lost manuscript might have proved to be. James A. Michener, who drew heavily upon *Ancient Tahiti* for early portions of his novel *Hawaii* and calls it "one of the world's most exciting ethnographic works—for the layman at least," adds: "The antecedents of Hawaii are explained in this work, and I consider it the best book ever written in Hawaii."

[4] JOHANNES C. ANDERSEN. *Myths and Legends of the Polynesians*. London: Harrap, 1929.

Charming myths, ranging from New Zealand to Central Polynesia to Hawaii, have been retold by a Danish scholar.

Modestly, the author says: "I came so late in the day that I have been able to gather but little, but I have tried to be a trumpet through which the musical Polynesian voice might make itself heard and attract attention to the power and personality behind the voice; and it is in this capacity that I have gathered together these gleanings of other men's harvests, so that my navigators and poets and orators, and savages, if the reader wills, may stand before him as do the Greeks of old, splendid even in the ruin of what they were." Sources acknowledged include James Cook, J. A. Moerenhout, Sir George Grey, W. W. Gill, Abraham Fornander, King Kalakaua, and S. Percy Smith.

Johannes Carl Andersen (1873–1962) was one of the most faithful students of Polynesian lore. Born in Denmark, he was librarian for many years at the Alexander Turnbull Library in Wellington, New Zealand. He edited the *Journal of the Polynesian Society* from 1925 to 1947. He was honored in 1944 by the award of the Royal Society Medal for Ethnology. During his long life Andersen published a number of articles and several books, such as *Polynesian Literature: Maori Poetry* (New Plymouth, New Zealand: T. Avery, 1946). A reprint of *Myths and Legends of the Polynesians*, retaining the romantic illustrations by Richard Wallwork, appeared in 1969 (Rutland, Vermont, and Tokyo: Charles E. Tuttle).

[5] SIR PETER H. BUCK ("Te Rangi Hiroa"). *Vikings of the Sunrise*. Philadelphia: Lippincott, 1938.

When the first Europeans arrived in the Pacific, they found that almost every one of the thousands of habitable islands in the so-called "Polynesian triangle", extending from Hawaii to Easter Island to New Zealand, had been occupied by descendants of the seafaring race of Polynesians, who had journeyed by canoe for thousands of miles from their ancient homeland in South China.

Still the most highly readable account of these remarkable voyages was written by Sir Peter H. Buck, who served on the staff of the Bernice P. Bishop Museum in Honolulu from 1927 to his death in 1951. Dr. Buck, born in New Zealand in 1880 and proud of the fact that his mother was of Maori stock, received an M.D. degree in 1910 and served in the Pacific as a medical officer in World War I. His archeological and ethnological studies were the basis for this volume which, although subject to some modification by researches after its publication, is a fascinating story. The reader shares the pride of the author in the achievements of the Polynesian canoe-builders and navigators who were the most skilled sailors in history, and whose tales of discovery of hidden atolls were accompanied by a reverence for nature and a store of legend that was pure poetry.

A softbound reprint of the original volume, retitled *Vikings of the Pacific*, was published in 1959 by the University of Chicago Press and the Cambridge University Press. Other general books that will be of interest to those seeking to know more of the mystery and accomplishments of the Polynesians are *Ancient Voyagers to Polynesia* by Andrew Sharp (Sydney: Angus & Robertson, 1963), which offers the theory that most if not all of the islands were populated by "accidental voyaging", and *The Island Civilizations of Polynesia* by Robert C. Suggs (New York: Mentor Books, 1960).

[6] WILLIAM S. STONE. *The Ship of Flame: A Saga of the South Seas.* New York: Alfred A. Knopf, 1945.

"Of all the races that have peopled the earth," says James Norman Hall, "there is none, perhaps, which at the period of its greatness, in proportion to its numbers, had preserved a larger, more varied treasure of mythical and legendary lore than the Polynesians. Among the tales handed down by word of mouth by countless generations was one concerning a monstrous Tridacna clam which, in the realm of legend, may well be compared, as an embodiment of the Spirit of Evil-without-a-Name, with the great white whale, Moby Dick. In *The Ship of Flame*, William S. Stone relates this legend for modern readers. It is a tale to remind one, with something of a shock of surprise and pleasure, that the Ages of Fable are not so lost in the Dark Backward of Time but that, under the right guidance, such as that of Mr. Stone, one may read and share, in an almost physical sense, the adventures of their legendary heroes."

Tetua, the bard of Tahiti, sits in his thatched house at Matavai Bay and tells the story. "Let him carry you to those distant days when the South Sea islands first rose like green jewels from the surrounding waters, to those days when his people walked hand in hand with mystery and wonder and great miracle. Let him tell you a tale which is always young in Tahitian memories, a tale of valor and of heroism; the story of the foremost of island kings, the first of island men. Rata was his name."

This story opens with young Rata, whose father King Tumunui leaves the lad behind when he sails for Revareva or Pitcairn. Rata's wish to be the tallest of men is granted by the gods. He wins at archery with the aid of his father's spirit, but discovers that the king is dead when the lone survivor, the steersman Hoa Pahi or Friend-of-the-Ship, floats ashore with news that the royal vessel had been destroyed by the giant Tridacna, Pahua. Rata decides to build a great canoe to avenge his father. In a secret valley the giant chief discovers a mighty tree that would form the hull of such a ship; but when he chops it down the elves knit the fibers overnight. Rata wins the help of the elves, who create Vaa-i-ama, the Ship of Flame, which descends to the sea on a rainbow. With his warrior crew, leaving his beloved Turia at Tahiti, Rata sails to the atolls where the monster lurks, overcoming dangers on the sea road. The last vengeful battle forms the climax of this saga. The story is told in crisp words pleasing to young and old listeners. The germ of the legend is found in Teuira Henry's *Ancient Tahiti* (see No. 3).

The Ship of Flame is sumptuously printed, as well as strikingly illustrated by Nicolas Mordvinoff, the author's friend in Papeete.

William Standish Stone was born in 1907 in Santa Barbara, California, of New England parents; his father was a chaplain in the United States Navy. Stone entered Harvard University in 1926. He became in 1929 a licensed airline transport pilot and instructor in a flying school in the Southwest. He had early begun the practice of law in Arizona, and in 1936 made his home in

Tahiti, where he was able to continue counseling on legal affairs. He was stricken with polio at the age of thirty but was able to swim by the island shores. Stone died in 1970 at Honolulu.

Stone began publishing his writing in 1935, and in Tahiti turned out eight books, dealing mainly with the South Seas. One of the best non-fiction volumes about his adopted island is *Tahiti Landfall* (New York: Morrow, 1946), which was the basis for the film "Pagan Love Song". Three books for children were published by Alfred A. Knopf. The novel *Two Came by Sea* (New York: Morrow, 1953; Sydney: Invincible Press, 1953) describes the conflict on the little Society Island of Atea between Pierre Lestrade, former member of the French resistance who comes to teach the gentle people there, and Alexandre Tissot, a man of Vichy who comes to rule over them. A deep understanding of the Polynesian mind and island living is revealed in this well-told story. Mr. Stone's latest book, *Idylls of the South Seas* (Honolulu: University of Hawaii Press, 1970), which again uses Tetua as narrator, returns to the legendary past of French Oceania which inspired *The Ship of Flame*.

[7] **KATHARINE LUOMALA.** *Voices on the Wind: Polynesian Myths and Chants*. Honolulu: Bishop Museum Press, 1955.

The best modern literary treatment of Polynesian poetry is presented in popular style by a leading Pacific anthropologist, Dr. Katharine Luomala.

"This book," says the author, "is another tale-bearing wind to carry beyond the islands the news about the favorite heroes and heroines of Polynesian tradition. . . . Storytellers have crisscrossed the southeastern Pacific with this heritage of tradition for the last two thousand years or more. It is so securely entrenched in the affections of narrators and listeners as to continue to be passed on orally and to survive into modern times. Wherever one goes, whether to Hawaii or to Tahiti or to New Zealand or to Samoa, one finds that most of these heroes and heroines are remembered. . . . What I have done in the following chapters, besides discuss some of the poetry and the training of the literary artists, is to choose certain of those Polynesian mythological characters who are generally regarded as having lived in the earlier period, in The Night of Tradition. To write about those whom both their Polynesian creators and I like best, and whose familiar biographies we never weary of hearing or telling once more, seems as good a basis as any for choosing from the thousands of Polynesian narratives which have been collected, translated, and published." A number of the chants included have been especially translated for this volume.

Chapters deal with chants and legends about the homelands, rebellion in Heaven and on earth, Maui the South Sea superman, two-faced Tinirau, the Menehunes or little people, Takahi the perfect chief, and Rata, irreverent vagabond. Sources given for South Sea literature include Peter H. Buck (see No. 5), Samuel H. Elbert, W. W. Gill (see No. 1), Hervé Audran, Bengt Danielsson (see No. 76), Edwin G. Burrows, Teuira Henry (see No. 3), Will Mariner (see No. 35), E. E. V. Collocott, Alfred Métraux, Kenneth P. Emory, Drury Lowe, E. W. Gifford, J. Frank Stimson, and S. Percy Smith. *Voices on the Wind* is delightfully illustrated in black and white by Joseph Feher.

Katharine Luomala was born in 1907 at Cloquet, Minnesota, and after attending the local schools obtained three degrees at the University of California, Berkeley, including a doctorate in anthropology. She did field work among the American Indians and in the Gilbert Islands of Micronesia. For some years she was editor of the *Journal of American Folklore*. She has obtained many research grants and is a member of a number of scholarly and professional societies. She is an honorary associate anthropologist of the Bernice P. Bishop Museum and professor of anthropology at the University of Hawaii. Monographs include *Maui-of-a-Thousand-Tricks: His Oceanic and European Biographers* (Honolulu: Bishop Museum Bulletin No. 198, 1949) and *The Menehune of Polynesia and Other Mythical Little People of Oceania* (Honolulu: Bishop Museum Bulletin No. 203, 1951).

[8] J. C. FURNAS. *Anatomy of Paradise: Hawaii and the Islands of the South Seas.* New York: William Sloane, 1948.

This venture into history, written by Joseph C. Furnas, born in 1905, in a magazinist style often verging on the flippant, represents a period when the sordid and seamy side of the Pacific past was presumed to be newsworthy. Despite his disclaimer, this book by Furnas is an "effort to debunk the South Seas in the brash manner of the 'twenties". It is useful for its odd, if unsupported, ironies, for its attempt to deal with a broad area, and for recognition of the contribution of literature to the legend of a Pacific paradise, as recognized in the lengthy list of "Sources Consulted". A better book by Furnas is *Voyage to Windward: The Life of Robert Louis Stevenson* (New York: William Sloane, 1951, available in Apollo Editions A-55).

[9] ALAN JOHN VILLIERS. *The Coral Sea.* London: Museum Press, 1949; New York: Scribner, 1949.

Captain Alan Villiers is known to sea lovers as author of a score of fine books and a world sailor.

Villiers, born in 1903 in Melbourne, Australia, after attending Essendon High School went to sea at the age of fifteen as apprentice in a sailing ship. He served for five years in British vessels, then switched to Scandinavian ships, whaling ships, and steamers. After a two-year stint as reporter in Hobart, Tasmania, he bought a half-interest in the bark *Parma* in 1931 and sailed in the "grain races" from Australia to England. He was bold enough in 1934 to buy the *Georg Stage*, a Danish training ship for more than fifty years, and man it with a crew consisting mainly of young adventure seekers. This ship, under the new name of *Joseph Conrad*, made a 60,000-mile cruise around the world under sail; she was the last full-rigged ship to round Cape Horn. The *Conrad* was in the Pacific from September, 1935, through July, 1936. The vessel was grounded on Wari Reef, near Samarai on the eastern tip of Papua, on April 3, 1936, but was able to kedge off and survive. The whole voyage is narrated in what has been called Villiers' best book, *The Cruise of the "Conrad"* (London: Hodder &

Stoughton, 1937; New York, Scribner, 1937). The *Conrad* was sold in 1937 and is now moored at the maritime museum at Mystic, Connecticut.

Villiers saw service during World War II as commander in the Royal Navy, and later sailed with Arabs in the Red Sea. He was master of the replica of the *Mayflower* which crossed the Atlantic in 1957 from Plymouth, England, to Plymouth, New England. He is a trustee of the National Maritime Museum and a fellow of the Royal Geographical Society. A recent book by him deals with the achievements of James Cook (see No. 22).

The Coral Sea is a stirring account of Pacific exploits, not limited to the empty area of the title. Villiers chronicles the periods from the adventures of explorers, buccaneers, blackbirders, and sandalwood traders to the sea battle of 1942, when the Japanese fleet got the first serious beating in its history. Villiers as an Australian was familiar with the stormy Coral Sea and sailed across it three times in the *Conrad*. Of the volume James A. Michener wrote: "I recommend this book to people who like to read about out-of-the-way places. Villiers recreates the Coral Sea with the affectionate touches of a true-born sailor."

[10] **ANTONIO PIGAFETTA.** *The First Voyage Round the World by Magellan (1518–1521)*. Translated from the accounts of Pigafetta and other contemporary writers. Accompanied by original documents, with notes and an introduction, by Lord Stanley of Alderley. London: Hakluyt Society, First Series, LII, 1874.

The first important voyage into the Pacific by Europeans was that of Fernando Magallanes—in Portuguese, Fernão Magalhães (*c.* 1480–1521), a mariner whose expedition left Spain on September 20, 1519, on what was to be the first circumnavigation of the globe. Magellan, after discovering and passing the strait that still bears his name, crossed the Pacific without encountering any land until he discovered the Marianas group on March 6, 1521. On March 16 he discovered the Philippine Islands, where he was killed on April 27 while taking part in a war between the chiefs of rival islands. The last ship, *Vittoria*, after wandering in the East Indies, rounded the Cape of Good Hope and returned to Spain under the command of Juan Sebastian del Cano just three years after its departure, laden with a valuable cargo of cloves.

The best account of the circumnavigation was written by an Italian member of the expedition, Antonio Pigafetta of Vicenza, who kept a journal of events. His original was lost, but a French abridgment fortunately had been made by Fabre at the request of the Emperor Charles V, and was published in Paris in 1525. In the same year an English translation, probably from the Italian, was published in London by Richard Wren. Pigafetta's account, more

The Spanish forces attempt to defeat the warriors of the Philippine island of Mactan. Magellan, their leader, is shown at lower right, receiving his death wound from the club of a defender.

or less abridged, appeared in various early collections, including one in which it was translated back into Italian from the French. A more recent edition than that of the Hakluyt Society is *Magellan's Voyage Around the World: the Original Text of the Ambrosian MS. with English Translation, Notes, and Bibliography*, edited by

James Alexander Robertson, 3 vol. (Cleveland, Ohio: A. H. Clark, 1906). Two excellent new translations are *Magellan's Voyage: A Narrative Account of the First Circumnavigation*, translated by R. A. Skelton (New Haven, Conn.: Yale University Press, 1969) and *The Voyage of Magellan: The Journal of Antonio Pigafetta*, translated by Paula Spurlin Paige (New York: Prentice-Hall, 1969).

Little is known of Pigafetta, "Patrician of Vicenza and Knight of Rhodes", but his clear and detailed account is basic to our knowledge of Magellan's achievements. A number of good biographies of Magellan are readily available. As stated by John Norman Leonard Baker in *A History of Geographical Discovery and Exploration* (London: Harrap; Boston: Houghton Mifflin, 1931): "Magellan succeeded where Columbus failed. He had proved that the world was round; he had also demonstrated the possibility of its circumnavigation. As a sailor, a geographer, an explorer, Magellan was a great man, greater perhaps than either Columbus or Da Gama, perhaps even, as has been suggested, 'the greatest of ancient and modern navigators'."

[11] **ANDREW SHARP.** *Adventurous Armada.* Christchurch, New Zealand: Whitcombe & Tombs, 1961.

After six years of preparation, a Spanish fleet of four ships left La Navidad on the Mexican west coast in November, 1564, to settle the East Indies. In command of almost four hundred men was Miguel López de Legazpi, a Basque who had become a wealthy merchant in Mexico City. Leader of the friars in the expedition was Legazpi's cousin, sixty-year-old Andrés de Urdaneta, who when younger had been to the Spice Islands on a voyage around the world from Spain. Urdaneta was a skilled pilot who later worked out the proper sailing route for the Manila galleons (see No. 12).

Legazpi's men visited islands in the Marshall group and had a brush with the Micronesian people of the "Ladrones" Islands, which he renamed the Marianas. The ships went further west, and conquered or pacified many of the Philippine Islands. The high point of Legazpi's life was the founding of Manila in May, 1571.

Thereafter that city was the center of Spanish occupation of the Philippines until 1898.

Eleven days out from La Navidad, the 40-ton *San Lucas* was separated and made its own historic voyage. Alonso de Arellano, its captain, running further south than Legazpi, discovered several islands in the Marshall and Caroline groups, including Truk. The *San Lucas* was later to be the first vessel to succeed in crossing the Pacific from west to east. After various adventures among the Philippine Islands, the tiny ship set out to return to America by way of high latitudes, beyond 40°, where no European keels had ever cut. The crew were smitten with scurvy, hordes of rats, and storms that tattered their sails. But twelve weeks after leaving the Philippines—a speedy as well as a pioneer voyage—the *San Lucas* sighted the California coast and ran down to her home port. Arellano had stumbled upon the return route that would be used by sailors in the Manila galleons for two and a half centuries thereafter, sometimes taking five or six months to complete it.

Andrew Sharp, born in New Zealand in 1906, took an advanced degree in the social sciences as a Rhodes scholar at Oxford. After a term in Burma in the Indian Civil Service he engaged in government work in New Zealand from 1939 to 1967. For many years he studied Pacific history. Some of his results are revealed in his *Ancient Voyagers in the Pacific* (Wellington, New Zealand: Polynesian Society Memoir No. 32, 1956; reprinted by Pelican Books, 1957, and, rewritten under the title of *Ancient Voyagers to Polynesia*, by Angus & Robertson, Sydney, 1963) and *The Discovery of the Pacific Islands* (London: Oxford University Press, 1960). Sharp makes a lively chronicle of the Legazpi voyage, using some untranslated Spanish documents. Written simply, *Adventurous Armada* tells of explorations, hardships at sea, conflicts with native people, marooning, mutiny, perilous passages, treasure seeking, and pacification of a broad archipelago.

[12] WILLIAM LYTLE SCHURZ. *The Manila Galleon*. New York: E. P. Dutton, 1939, 1959.

The galleons of Spain crossed the Pacific between Manila in the Philippines and Acapulco in Mexico for two and a half centuries.

The first sailed in 1565, the same year in which St. Augustine, oldest city in the United States, was founded. The last sailed in 1815, the year when Andrew Jackson won the Battle of New Orleans. Between those years, more than a thousand of these lumbering, armed cargo vessels made the voyage of many months, enduring the perils of storm, disease, and piracy. No other line of ships has endured so long.

The galleons carried from Manila, the depot for the Oriental trade, all the luxuries of Asia and the Spice Islands. They returned laden with silver from the mines of Mexico and South America. To find American ports for the weary galleons, the original explorers and settlers of California set out. Perils were many. The ocean claimed dozens of these argosies, thousands of their crews, and many millions of treasure. The mutiny of the *San Gerónimo* rivals in drama that of the *Bounty*. The galleons were the most coveted prizes of corsairs—four ships were captured by English pirates or privateers. Nevertheless, the precious trade continued, hauling the wealth of Asia across half the world, holding together the empire of Spain.

Dr. Schurz's study, the result of many years of research, is a fascinating account of an enduring enterprise. It not only gives the facts about all aspects of the galleon trade, but is virtually a history of the Pacific Ocean during the centuries. Chapters are devoted to Chinese, Japanese, Portuguese, Spanish, English, and Dutch adventurers in the region. "This is a sumptuous banquet of glamor, excitement, and thrills," says Professor Howard Mumford Jones. "The reader is given a glowing and unforgettable panorama of one of the most romantic ventures in history." The browser is immediately swept into reading whole chapters.

William Lytle Schurz, historian, journalist, and former State Department official, was born in South Lebanon, Ohio. He was educated at Oberlin College and the University of California, where he fell under the sway of the historians then revealing that the history of Spanish America was highly pertinent to the history of the United States. Dr. Schurz not only taught Latin-American history at several universities but served as diplomat, explorer, commercial agent, export manager to a large manufacturing firm, and economic adviser to a Latin-American government. *The Manila Galleon* is the only one of his several books that deals primarily with the Pacific.

[13] WILLIAM AMHERST and BASIL THOMSON (eds.). *The Discovery of the Solomon Islands by Alvaro Mendaña de Neira in 1568.* 2 vol. London: Hakluyt Society, Second Series, VI, 1901.

Alvaro de Mendaña, young nephew of the viceroy of Peru, headed an expedition of two ships which left Callao in 1567 to seek two rich islands that, according to Inca legend, lay to the westward. Among the hundred and fifty men were four Franciscan friars who were supposed to convert the pagans. After finding only two small islands during eighty days of sailing, the explorers, in August, 1568, blundered upon the high islands of a Melanesian group. Fighting broke out between the Spaniards and the cannibal inhabitants of islands which Mendaña named Santa Ysabel, Malaita, San Cristóbal, and Guadalcanal—where the small settlement of the Spaniards was set afire by vengeful Melanesian survivors of a massacre. Deciding to return to Peru was less easy than making the voyage. The crews endured calms, a tremendous hurricane, and starvation and scurvy, but after thirteen months at sea in the North Pacific, the two ships returned to Callao.

The argonauts on this voyage, according to the various accounts herein, found no gold or lands of wealth, but the legend grew up that Mendaña had discovered the fabled islands whence King Solomon had brought the adornments for his temple at Jerusalem. The second voyage of Mendaña in 1595 (see No. 14) and other voyages by men of several nations were designed to rediscover the Solomon Islands, but these were not seen again by Europeans for two centuries.

[14] SIR CLEMENTS MARKHAM (ed.). *The Voyages of Pedro Fernández de Quirós.* 2 vol. London: Hakluyt Society, Second Series, XIV, XV, 1904.

Quirós, one of the best navigators to serve Spain in the Pacific, was born in the Portuguese town of Evora around 1563 and died in 1615 at Panama, on his way to what he hoped would be the leadership of another exploring expedition in the South Sea.

His skill qualified Quirós to serve as chief pilot for the Mendaña fleet that left Peru in 1595, which discovered the Marquesas and

Santa Cruz groups and ended in disaster. Mendaña, now in his fifties, was married to a greedy wife with many greedy relatives who also went along on this impressive colonizing expedition. Despite the peacemaking efforts of Quirós, murder and mutiny broke out, Mendaña died, and only one ship of the fleet limped into Manila, bearing about a hundred survivors out of some four hundred that had left Peru.

Making his way back to that country in June, 1597, Quirós proposed to lead another expedition. After going to Rome and obtaining encouragement from Pope Clement VIII, Quirós managed after more than eight years to sail from Peru once more to set up a New Jerusalem in Melanesia.

Natives of New Guinea as portrayed in the log of the 1606 voyage of Quirós.

Six Franciscan friars went with the three hundred sailors manning three ships that sailed toward the end of 1605. Quirós became more and more fanatical about his holy mission, and in the New Hebrides, in April, 1606, attempted to colonize Terra Austrialia [*sic*] del Espíritu Santo, named for the Spanish king, who was also Archduke of Austria. But threats of mutiny arose, his flagship was separated in a storm from his surviving consort, and

Quirós, ill and worried, ordered a discouraged return to Peru. A smaller vessel, under the command of Luís Váez de Torres, headed west and discovered the reef-strewn strait named for him, lying between New Guinea and the northernmost cape of the Australian continent. Quirós spent eight years back in Spain, writing many "memorials" pleading for another chance to settle the islands he had discovered, but the days of important Spanish exploration in the South Seas passed with the death of this capable navigator, who has been called "the Columbus of the Pacific".

This Markham edition could well be replaced by a more modern translation. The first and third narratives, first published in Madrid in 1876, were probably written by the young poet Luís de Belmonte Bermudez. The later voyage is translated and edited by Celsus Kelly, S.J., in *La Austrialia del Espíritu Santo* (London: Hakluyt Society, Second Series, CXXVI, CXXVII, 1966). The part played by Quirós in the expedition of 1595 is covered by James A. Michener and A. Grove Day in *Rascals in Paradise* (London: Secker & Warburg, 1957; New York: Random House, 1957), Chapter VI. Two excellent novels deal with this expedition, somewhat altering the facts. These are *The Islands of Unwisdom* (London: Cassell, 1950; New York: Doubleday, 1949) by Robert Graves, British novelist and poet, and *The Quality of Quirós* (Indianapolis, Ind.: Bobbs-Merrill, 1955) by an American, Robert Raynolds. The expedition of 1606 inspired a lengthy poem, *Captain Quirós* (Sydney: Angus & Robertson, 1964), by an Australian, James McAuley.

[15] WILLIAM DAMPIER. *A New Voyage Round the World . . .* London: J. Knapton, 1697.

William Dampier (1651–1715), "pirate and hydrographer", was one of the earliest of the great travel writers who put the Pacific on the literary map. He made five voyages in that ocean, and in his later years was the most experienced British navigator of the time. He stands alone as a Pacific explorer between Francis Drake and James Cook; and as an observant, practical scientist he influenced men like Matthew Flinders, Charles Darwin, and Matthew Maury.

William was born of solid Somerset yeoman stock. With only slight schooling, he had a genius for observing and recording details. After early voyages to France, Newfoundland, and Java, he enlisted in the British Navy but was discharged for illness. He managed a Jamaican plantation and after some sailing in the Caribbean tried his luck as a logwood cutter in the Bay of Campeche, Mexico. From there it was easy to drift into the buccaneering lay. Dampier at the age of twenty-nine was in the advance guard of the army of pirates that marched across the Isthmus of Panama in 1680, hoping to repeat the success of Henry Morgan's men, who sacked and burned the golden city of Panama a decade earlier. The later party failed to breach the stone walls of the rebuilt city, and Dampier sailed "on the account" with the notorious Captain Bartholomew Sharp in the captured *Trinity*.

Dampier naturally wrote little about his first voyage as a Pacific buccaneer, but information about the period and later ones is available in the library of piracy. After a year spent in poverty and "trouble" in Virginia, Will signed on with a Captain John Cook. The crew captured a neutral Danish ship and rechristened her the *Bachelor's Delight*. They rounded Cape Horn on St. Valentine's Day, 1684, and after some desultory captures joined a fleet of English and French buccaneers for another attempt

Rescue of William, a Caribbean Indian who had been marooned on Juan Fernández for four years, by crew of the *Bachelor's Delight*.

against Panama. On August 25, Dampier shifted to the *Cygnet* under Captain Charles Swan, hoping to persuade him to attempt the capture of a Manila galleon off Mexico, a feat achieved by Thomas Cavendish in 1587. But the galleon was warned away by fishermen and Swan lost fifty men during an attack on an inland town in Mexico.

Piloted by Dampier, the *Cygnet*, accompanied by a small captured bark, sailed the thousands of miles to Guam, with the crew starving on a ration of half a pint of dried corn daily. The people at Guam, mistreated by buccaneers, warned the Manila galleon to steer clear of the island. The crew mutinied when Swan and thirty-six other men were ashore, and sailed off to cruise aimlessly through the East Indies with Dampier at the helm. They were the first Englishmen to visit Australia, but were unimpressed by their six weeks on the coast of what is still named Dampier Land. The future author's description of the aboriginals of "New Holland" probably inspired Jonathan Swift to write about Gulliver among the Yahoos.

At his request, Dampier was put ashore on the Nicobar Islands in the Bay of Bengal and after hardships made his way to Sumatra. Despite fever and dysentery he sailed up the "Tonkin River" and explored the region today known as North Viet Nam. After a voyage to Malacca and a period as master gunner at the English trading post of Bencoolen on Sumatra, Dampier returned home after a twelve-year odyssey. He spent his time usefully, and the journal that he had kept beside him through many adventures was published in the spring of 1697.

A New Voyage Round the World brought fame to the ex-buccaneer. The British Admiralty accepted in due time his proposal that he command a naval vessel to chart the continent later called Australia. This exploring craft was a fifth-rater previously classed as a fire ship. The saga of the *Roebuck* is an amazing story of trouble and survival. Dampier explored the south coast of New Guinea, discovered New Britain, "St. George's Bay", and Dampier Strait. His seamanship enabled the leaky vessel to avoid foundering until she neared Ascension Island, almost the only land in the South Atlantic, which he gained without the loss of a man. Although condemned on his return by a court-martial for mistreating his lieutenant, Dampier was soon called to voyage again. During the War of the Spanish Succession he was appointed to command the privateer *St. George*, which sailed in May, 1703, with a smaller consort, the *Cinque Ports*, to harry the French and Spanish. After some successes off South America, Dampier again failed to capture a Manila galleon off Mexico. He was hit by mutiny and desertion, and when he and his loyal men reached the East Indies in a captured ship, he was imprisoned because his letter of marque, identifying him as a lawful privateer, had been stolen by his mate, John Clipperton.

Somehow Dampier returned to England, again without a penny in his pocket. Although he was now fifty-six, he was still in demand as a pilot. The success of the Woodes Rogers expedition (see No. 16) was due in no small part to Dampier's skill as a navigator. Will returned to England with claims to part of the huge booty brought back by Rogers, but died in debt, despite some income from his books.

Shortly after the *Roebuck* sailed in January, 1699, Dampier's second book, *Voyages and Descriptions*, appeared (London: Knapton, 1699). It contained a supplement to the voyage around the world, a voyage to Campeche, and his valuable "Discourse on the Trade Winds". His *A Voyage to New Holland* appeared in two parts (I, London: J. Knapton, 1703; II, same, 1709). The last work written by him was a fiery *Vindication . . .* (London: Knapton, 1707), answering attacks by two of his men on his behavior in command of the *St. George*.

Tributes to Dampier as a scientist and writer have been given by many, including Samuel Taylor Coleridge, Admiral James Burney, and sailor-laureate John Masefield—who edited an excellent two-volume collection of Dampier's voyages (London: E. Grant Richards, 1906). A biography is Clennell Wilkinson's *Dampier: Explorer and Buccaneer* (New York: Harper & Bros., 1929). A recent account of Dampier in the Pacific is A. Grove Day, *Adventurers of the Pacific* (New York: Meredith Press, 1969, Chapter 5). A novel about the *Roebuck* voyage is Alan Chester's *Brother Captain* (London: P. Davies, 1964).

[16] WOODES ROGERS. *A Cruising Voyage Round the World . . . Begun in 1708 and Finished in 1711.* London: A. Bell & B. Lintot, 1712.

Captain Woodes Rogers (1679?–1732), in command of the *Duke* and *Duchess*, privateers on a round-the-world foray "against His Majesty's enemies, the French and the Spaniards", wrote this brisk and at times quaintly humorous "buccaneering classic", as it has been termed by the *Dictionary of National Biography*. He maintained order throughout the circumnavigation, despite raffish crews and officers who were often inclined to mutiny. His chief pilot was William Dampier (see No. 15). Rogers was one of the few privateersmen who actually captured the coveted galleon laden with silver on its way from Mexico to Manila.

The popularity of this account is attested by frequent reprints. A second edition, corrected, appeared in London in 1718, and others in 1722 and 1726. A handy modern edition was published by the Seafarer's Library (London: Cassell, 1928), with introduction and notes by G. E. Manwaring. Rogers' journal was printed with notes under the title of *Life Aboard a British Privateer in the Time of Queen Anne* (London: Chapman & Hall, 1894).

A lesser account of this voyage was written by Edward Cooke, captain of the *Duchess*, and entitled *A Voyage to the South Sea and Round the World, 1708–1711* (London: H.M. for B. Lintot & R. Gosling, 1712). This was rushed into print in an attempt to anticipate the book by Woodes Rogers. Cooke's account, in which the latter part of the voyage was compressed into a few pages, was soon supplemented by a second volume which attempted to repair omissions.

A journalistic retelling of the voyage of the *Duke* and *Duchess* is given by Fleming MacLeish and Martin L. Krieger in *Fabulous Voyage* (London: Gollancz, 1963; the American title is *The Privateers*, New York: Random House, 1962).

The book by Rogers is fascinating not only in itself but because during the voyage the captain rescued the original Robinson Crusoe. This was Alexander Selkirk, a contentious Scotsman who had been marooned on Más a Tierra in the Juan Fernández group in 1704 by Captain Thomas Stradling of the privateer *St. George*. Rogers gave the first account to the world of the Selkirk story.

When Selkirk reached London he was interviewed by the essayist Richard Steele and issued a pamphlet about his adventures while living for four years and four months on his island in the company of cats and goats. He then put his papers in the hands of Daniel Defoe, whose imagination transformed Selkirk's story into the immortal novel *The Life and Strange Surprizing Adventures of Robinson Crusoe* (London: W. Taylor, 1719). Among the many items concerning Selkirk may be mentioned *Crusoe's Island* (New York: Harper, 1864) by John Ross Browne, a description of Más a Tierra.

[17] **GEORGE SHELVOCKE.** *A Voyage Round the World by Way of the Great South Sea* . . . London: J. Senex, 1726.

Shelvocke was head of the last privateering expedition into the Pacific. He was a cheat and a pirate, but his book—an attempted justification to ward off charges by his defrauded backers—is a fascinating account of voyaging and fighting.

George Shelvocke belonged to an ancient Shropshire family, and was born, probably at Deptford, in 1675. He entered the Royal Navy at about the age of fifteen, and rose to be second lieutenant of a flagship. During peacetime, he fell into great poverty, and was rescued by his former purser, one of a group of men who had fitted out two privateering vessels to attack Spanish commerce in the South Seas, in anticipation of a war that was declared in December, 1718. These vessels were the *Success* of 350 tons, with thirty-six guns and 180 men, and the *Speedwell* of 200 tons, twenty-two guns, and 106 men. Before departure the owners, discontented by months of delay, demoted Shelvocke to the smaller *Speedwell* and put John Clipperton in command of the *Success*. Clipperton had twice made voyages to the coasts of Chile and Peru and had been William Dampier's mate in 1704 (see No. 15). Neither captain wished to take orders from the other, and each went off on his own account very soon. Both were given sailing orders, letters of marque, and copies of the recently published book by Woodes Rogers (see No. 16).

In the Pacific, Shelvocke captured several prizes, including one off Peru laden with "cormorants' dung", used for fertilizer—he gives the earliest printed report on the guano industry. The most disastrous event of the voyage was the inexplicable wreck of the *Speedwell* in a gale on May 25, 1720, on the rocky shore of Más a Tierra, one of the Juan Fernández Islands. The crew decided that shipboard discipline no longer prevailed; they organized as a voting group to divide the plunder, but Shelvocke salvaged some dollars and silver bars for himself. After two weeks he persuaded the men to start building a new ship, using tree trunks and timbers from the wreck. This clumsy vessel, the *Recovery*, was found to be too small to hold all the survivors, and a number were left behind as Crusoes. After six weeks the privateers captured a 200-ton Spanish ship and transferred to her. Off the Mexican coast, Shelvocke was chased by a familiar vessel. It was the *Success*, which he had not seen since leaving Plymouth two years before.

Clipperton separated once more after a few days and headed across the Pacific on a disastrous voyage; he was almost captured in the harbor of Guam, and sold the *Success* at Macao for a fraction of her value. With an ill-gotten hoard of money, he reached his home in Ireland in June, 1722, but died there a week later. Shelvocke captured a bigger Spanish vessel, the *Sacra Familia*, and laden with looted provisions followed Clipperton's track across the broad Pacific and sold the stolen ship to the Chinese. At Canton he divided the prize money of the voyage among thirty-three surviving men (Shelvocke lists more than eighty Englishmen of his company "as died, deserted, or were taken or killed by the enemy"), allotting himself more than £2,500. He cheated his crew by holding back a sack of golden doubloons he had hidden in his cabin.

Arrived in England as a passenger after three years and seven months of travel, he found he had retained a fortune of more than £7,000. He was dismissed on a charge of piracy because of lack of evidence, but was at once arrested by the cheated men who had backed the expedition. Shelvocke escaped from the King's Bench Prison and fled to France, where his biased but exciting account was written. A purged and refined edition was republished in 1757 by his son George, who had made the voyage with his father. A reprint of the original, with introduction and notes by W. G. Perrin, appeared in the Seafarers' Library (London: Cassell, 1928). A companion to the Shelvocke book is *Voyage*

Round the World . . . (London: T. Combes, 1728), by William Betagh, who had started out as captain of the marines in the *Speedwell* and whose animosity toward Shelvocke results in a lively and very different version of the voyage. The Shelvocke and Betagh narratives are both included in *A Privateer's Voyage Around the World* (London: Jonathan Cape, 1930) in the Travellers' Library.

Shelvocke's description of California borrows from the account by Woodes Rogers. He adds, however, the first printed intimation of the existence of gold in that region. A passage in Shelvocke sparked a literary inspiration. While attempting to round gloomy Cape Horn amid a succession of contrary gales, where only one bird was seen—a black albatross, Simon Hatley, Shelvocke's second captain, "observing, in one of his melancholy fits, that this bird was always hovering near us, imagined, from his color, that it might be some ill omen. . . . He, after some fruitless attempts, at length shot the albatross." William Wordsworth suggested in 1797 to Samuel Taylor Coleridge, when they were discussing the composition of "The Rime of the Ancient Mariner", that the crime for which the mariner was to be punished might be Hatley's act in Shelvocke's book, which Wordsworth had been reading a day or two before. "Suppose", said Wordsworth, "you represent him as having killed one of these birds on entering the South Sea, and that the tutelary spirits of these regions take upon them to avenge the crime." Thus a high point in a poem written many years later was one result of Shelvocke's piratical foray in the South Seas.

[18] **GEORGE ANSON.** *A Voyage Round the World in the Years 1740, 1, 2, 3, 4; compiled from Papers and Other Materials, of the Right Honourable George Lord Anson, and Published Under His Direction by Richard Walter, M.A., Chaplain of His Majesty's Ship the "Centurion" in That Expedition.* London: printed for the author by John and Paul Knapton, 1748.

Commodore George Anson (1697–1762), commanding a squadron of eight vessels and almost a thousand men, set out in 1740 to attack Spanish shipping and, in particular, a squadron under Don

José Pizarro sent to reinforce Spanish possessions in the South Seas. Two of the ships were lost attempting to round Cape Horn and another, the *Wager*, was driven ashore and lost on the Chilean coast. Two other ships were in such bad shape that they were abandoned in the Pacific. Many of the crew had been badly chosen for a circumnavigation, and scurvy took a heavy toll. By the summer of 1741, Anson found that his fleet was reduced to one ship, and almost two-thirds of his original force had died, leaving only 335 survivors to crowd into the flagship, the *Centurion*. In mid-November they attacked the town of Paita in northern Peru, and with only slight losses looted and set fire to it. Off Mexico, Anson missed a Manila galleon laden with treasure of the Orient, and sailed across the Pacific seeking another.

Reinforcing his depleted crew with a score of Asians recruited at Macao, Anson sighted his prey, a galleon delayed through fear of his attack, off the Philippine island of Samar. The great battle between the *Centurion* and *Nuestra Señora de Covadonga* on June 20, O.S., 1743, resulted in a rich victory. After Anson's return by way of the Cape of Good Hope, the captured treasure was paraded through London in thirty-two wagons. Spanish commerce in the Pacific never recovered from this raid, and maps captured on the *Covadonga*, supplemented by observations of the *Centurion's* officers, cleared the way for future British expeditions on Pacific routes.

The main source of information on the voyage is the book compiled by Chaplain Richard Walter (1716?–1785). He was given a B.A. degree by Cambridge University in 1738. Even though "a puny, weakly man, pale, and of a low stature", he was often called to serve with the others in the working of the ship. He was given permission, in December, 1742, to leave the *Centurion* at Macao and return to England. His book was written with the advice of Commodore Anson, and contained forty-two maps and other illustrations drawn by Lieutenant Piercy Brett. Brett and Justinian Nutt, master of the *Centurion*, provided navigational notes. Although Walter was not on board during the action with the Manila galleon nor for dealings with the Chinese authorities at Canton, these events are described at length. The book, published in 1748, was immensely popular; four reprintings came before the year was out, and by 1781 there were sixteen in English and other languages. It was included in Everyman's Library in

1911 (London: Dent; New York: Dutton) with an introduction by John Masefield. An edition limited to 1,500 copies, with a prefatory note by G. S. Laird Clowes, appeared in 1928 (London: Martin Hopkinson; Boston: Charles E. Lauriat).

Walter's rival chronicler was the ship's "teacher of the mathematics", Pascoe Thomas. His book is entitled *A True and Impartial Journal of a Voyage to the South Seas and Round the Globe in His Majesty's Ship the "Centurion" under the Command of Commodore George Anson* (London: printed and sold by various booksellers in Great Britain, 1745). Thomas padded his journal with borrowings from earlier books, and managed to get out his volume three years before Walter's more official account. A third source on the voyage is the first published—*An Authentic Journal . . . by John Phillips, Midshipman of the "Centurion"* (London: printed for J. Robinson at the Golden Lion in Ludgate Street, 1744). No person of that name appears on the muster; the pseudonym may have been used because the book contains the story of John Bulkeley, a warrant officer on the *Wager* and a ringleader in a mutiny, whose court martial was still under consideration when "John Phillips" published his volume. It was likewise popular and was at once pirated by two British publishers under a different title, and written "by an Officer of the Fleet".

The standard account of the circumnavigation is *Commodore Anson's Voyage into the South Seas and Around the World* (London and Toronto: Heinemann, 1934) by Henry Boyle Townshend Somerville, Vice-Admiral, C.M.G. Two entertaining novels about the adventure are Francis van Wyck Mason's *Manila Galleon* (Boston: Little, Brown, 1961) and *Jenkins' Ear* by Odell and Willard Shepard (New York: Macmillan, 1951), a narrative attributed to Horace Walpole.

[19] GEORGE ROBERTSON. *The Discovery of Tahiti: a Journal of the Second Voyage of H.M.S. "Dolphin" Round the World, 1766–1768.* Edited by Hugh Carrington. London: Hakluyt Society, Second Series, XCVIII, 1948.

A round-the-world expedition consisting of the copper-bottomed 32-gun frigate *Dolphin* under Captain Samuel Wallis

(1728–1795) and the 14-gun sloop *Swallow* under Captain Philip Carteret left London on July 8, 1766. After a four-month battle to pass the Strait of Magellan, the *Dolphin* was then separated from the little *Swallow*, whose log on her slow return to England tells one of the great stories of survival (see No. 20). The *Dolphin* cruised westward through the reef-studded Tuamotu Archipelago and on June 19, 1767, sighted the peaks of Tahiti. Following a brush with Polynesian warriors in canoes, the *Dolphin* entered Matavai Bay and the officers and crew were greeted by "Queen Oberea". For a month they refreshed themselves at Tahiti, a name even now synonymous with a South Sea paradise. Thereafter Wallis sighted several other islands and on his way to the Marianas discovered the group that his men named for him.

George Robertson, master of the *Dolphin* for the two-year voyage, began serving at about the age of thirty as master's mate in the Royal Navy in 1761 and, after successive promotions, commanded several British vessels during the American Revolution. On the circumnavigation, both Wallis and First Lieutenant William Clarke were ill much of the time, and the success of the expedition can be credited mainly to Sub-Lieutenant Tobias Furneaux and to Robertson the master. Robertson's journal extends from June 24, 1766, to August 17, 1767, when the *Dolphin* was off the group newly named the Wallis Islands. This very personal journal, written in direct and unadorned English and marked by his engaging orthography, is a rugged record of the historic first contact with a celebrated haven. Carrington's editing is superb, with a bibliography and plates added.

A selection from the journal appears in *An Account of the Discovery of Tahiti*, edited with an introduction by Oliver Warner, with wood engravings by Robert Gibbings (London: The Folio Society, 1955, printed for members only). Wallis's own journal appears in *An Account of the Voyages . . . for Making Discoveries in the Southern Hemisphere* by John Hawkesworth, 3 vol. (London: W. Strahan and T. Cadell, 1773).

A retelling of part of Robertson's adventures is found in Newton Allan Rowe, *Voyage to the Amorous Islands: the Discovery of Tahiti* (London: André Deutsch, 1955).

[20] PHILIP CARTERET. *Voyage Round the World, 1766–1769.* Edited by Helen Wallis. 2 vol. London: Hakluyt Society, Second Series, Nos. CXXIV, CXXV, 1965.

The saga of the little *Swallow*, consort of Wallis's *Dolphin* (see No. 19), has recently been published in detail. Previously the only record in print was that in the collection of Dr. John Hawkesworth, *An Account of the Voyages Undertaken by the Order of His Present Majesty for Making Discoveries in the Southern Hemisphere . . .* 3 vol. (London: W. Strahan and T. Cadell, 1773). Seldom has a vessel of the size and condition of the sloop *Swallow* achieved a circumnavigation or made more discoveries in the Pacific.

Even before Carteret sailed from England, he could not believe that he and his men were supposed to go around the world in this twenty-year-old, sixth-rate sloop. The thought that the *Swallow* would not be able to keep up with the speedy, copper-sheathed *Dolphin* did not occur to the Lords of the Admiralty, and all the stores and trade goods were loaded on the larger vessel—a failure that was to cause no little grief to Carteret's men.

The two ships sailed on August 22, 1766, and Carteret, who had returned to England in May from a voyage around the world in the *Dolphin* under "Foul-weather Jack" Byron, led the way through the Strait of Magellan. The two ships spent almost four months making the passage into the Pacific, and at once the *Dolphin* shot ahead of the *Swallow* in stormy weather and left the little vessel, a floundering hulk, to make her way alone. Carteret might well have given up the Pacific attempt, but his men agreed to work the ship home around the world. They survived evil weather. Desperate for water, some of the men swam ashore through boiling surf at the island of Más Afuera with casks strapped to their backs. Carteret was the first navigator after Quirós (1606) to take the route south of the trade-wind belt. He discovered Pitcairn and several other small islands. A fourth of Carteret's crew came down with scurvy, and he and his first mate were ill; in an unexplored region they were the only men on board, aside from the sailing master, who knew how to navigate. They stumbled, on August 12, 1767, upon the Santa Cruz group, which had not been seen since Mendaña died there in 1595—almost two centuries previously. Carteret also rediscovered the Solomon Islands. Further west, he found on August 26 that what Dampier had called St. George's Bay was really a channel. Leaving Dampier's New Britain to the south, Carteret gave to the coast north of him the name of New Ireland. Beyond, he found and named New Hanover and the Admiralty group.

The *Swallow*, with drooping wings, reached the Celebes. Out of a crew of ninety, thirteen had died and fifty others were dying. For fear of contagion, the Dutch officer who came aboard refused to land the sick or even permit the ship to enter harbor. Carteret had to threaten to run the *Swallow* ashore and fight the Dutch to the death before he was allowed the aid he so badly needed. The return of the *Swallow* on March 20, 1769, to England, two years and seven months after her departure around the world, was a miracle of seamanship that should not be overshadowed by the stories of more frequently lauded voyagers. Carteret retired in 1794 as a rear admiral and died in 1796.

A month before Carteret reached home, in mid-Atlantic, an officer from a French ship came aboard the *Swallow* and asked many acute questions. Not until later did Carteret discover that the vessel was the *Boudeuse* under Louis Antoine de Bougainville, who had been trailing him around the Pacific and who was amazed by Carteret's explorations and courage in achieving so much in a small, backward ship.

The availability of the Carteret records is enhanced by the editorship of Dr. Helen Wallis of the British Museum Map Room. Of these two volumes a reviewer, Colin Jack-Hinton, says that they "reflect a thoroughly scholarly approach to the material with which the editor has had to deal, a prodigious amount of research, and a detailed knowledge of the academic questions of discovery, cartography, textual detail, and comparison. The Editorial is a stylish, substantial, and very readable piece of work, which is adequately reinforced by the detailed footnotes and other editorial comments which appear elsewhere in the book. Carteret has been well served" (*Journal of Pacific History*, I, 1966, 233).

[21] ROBERT LANGDON. *Tahiti: Island of Love.* London: Cassell, 1959; 3rd ed., Sydney: Pacific Publications, 1968.

The best popular chronicle in English of the most romantic—and most beautiful—Pacific isle is Robert Langdon's *Tahiti: Island of Love.* The crews of both Samuel Wallis's *Dolphin* and the two ships of co-discoverer Louis Antoine de Bougainville soon made the girls of Tahiti the dream of every romantic follower of Jean-Jacques Rousseau. Bougainville, who often thought he had been transported to the Garden of Eden, called Tahiti *La Nouvelle Cythère*, island of the love goddess Aphrodite herself. The reports of later visitors, from James Cook to the most recent jet globe-trotters, give a mounting appreciation of the charms of this Polynesian paradise.

"My book is not a history of Tahiti," announces the author in his introduction. "It might best be described as a chronological narrative of the events which have made the island famous. Naturally, there is a good deal of history in the book." He remarks, quite exactly, that "the literature on Tahiti is amazingly vast. The information I needed was buried in hundreds of different, and often unexpected, places. . . . For the chapter called 'The Romance of Atimaono', for example, I read every newspaper published in Tahiti between 1862 and 1875, all the British consular correspondence, numerous travel books, and a great deal of other material." The results of research have been well digested into a smooth narrative that tells as much about the visitors and sojourners in this South Sea Arcadia as about the Polynesian inhabitants who have welcomed them for the past two centuries.

Robert Adrian Langdon was born in 1924 at Adelaide, South Australia, and educated at the high school in that city. He served during World War II in the Royal Australian Navy. After six years of civilian travel in many parts of the world, working at various jobs, he first visited Tahiti in 1953 as a fireman on a New Zealand passenger liner. Back in Adelaide, while employed as a journalist and free-lance writer, he continued to seek information on Tahiti's past. He became a staff writer for the *Pacific Islands Monthly* in Sydney in 1962 and assistant editor from 1964 to 1967. He traveled extensively through the South Seas and wrote numerous articles on the exploration, history, and archeology of the Pacific. Thereafter he was appointed executive officer of the Pacific Manuscripts Bureau in the Australian National Library at Canberra. This bureau, a joint endeavor of five of the world's major Pacific research libraries, is charged with obtaining, preserving, and disseminating unpublished material dealing with Pacific history.

[22] JAMES COOK. *The Journals of Captain James Cook on His Voyages of Discovery*, edited by J. C. Beaglehole. 3 vol. and portfolio. London: Hakluyt Society, 1955, 1961, 1967.

"The greatest explorer-seaman the world has known", in the words of Captain Alan Villiers, was James Cook (1728–1789), a self-made navigator and discoverer who spent the last decade of his life charting much of the Pacific from the Arctic to the Antarctic Circles. When he entered this ocean in 1769, much of the map of the Southern Hemisphere was covered with a spreading, imaginary continent called "Terra Australis Incognita". After his untimely death in the Hawaiian Islands, which he had discovered, his rivals said admiringly of him: "He has done so much that he has left us nothing to do but to admire his work." As Cook's latest editor concludes: "The map of the Pacific is his ample panegyric."

James Cook was born in a humble farm cottage in Yorkshire, but at an early age followed the call of the sea. He toiled before the mast on "cats" hauling coals from Newcastle around the North Sea—a hard school that toughened him for longer voyages in similar vessels in future. He also trained his mind to learn mathematics and the art of navigation, and thus rose to the rank of master's mate in the Royal Navy. He served off American shores during the Seven Years' War, and piloted the fleet below Quebec before General James Wolfe captured that town. For four years he mapped the coasts of Newfoundland. When, at the request of the Royal Society, a ship was to be fitted out to send to the South Seas to make astronomical observations, the Admiralty was wise enough to choose James Cook to command her.

Promoted to the rank of lieutenant, the tall, gawky seaman with the sharp eye for details helped to pick the proper ship. She was a

368-ton bark similar to those in the coal trade. Christened *Endeavour*, she was the first vessel ever assigned to a purely scientific voyage. Her crew of 94 was supplemented by a group of scientists led by young Joseph Banks, later to be president of the Royal Society for more than thirty years. In addition to the aims of science, Cook was secretly ordered to search for Terra Australis Incognita, and also to find suitable harbors in the Pacific for British naval bases.

The voyage of the *Endeavour* is one of the great adventures of mankind. She beat around Cape Horn late in January, 1769, and on April 13 anchored in Matavai Bay at Tahiti, which Samuel Wallis (see No. 19) had recommended as a suitable place for observations of the planets. Cook himself was one of the three men who watched the transit of Venus across the face of the sun. His landing place has ever since been called Point Venus. Cook was then free to go exploring. He made a precise map of Tahiti, and cruised for three weeks among the islands to the northwest, aided by a high priest named Tupuia who was a skilled voyager. To the entire group Cook gave the name of Society Islands, in honor of the Royal Society that had backed the expedition.

Heading southward, he sighted on October 7 the northern island of New Zealand. Abel Tasman had spent part of one day off the shore of the South Island; Cook spent six months making a circuit of New Zealand and trying to become friends with the cannibal Maoris of those islands. Thereafter he did what no man had ever done before: he ordered his ship to sail westward across the stormy Tasman Sea. First Lieutenant Zachariah Hicks sighted land on April 20, 1770. It was the southeastern corner of the continent of Australia, which was unknown to the world except for its barren western shores, called New Holland by the Dutch voyagers. Cook named his discovery New South Wales.

Following the coast northward, Cook found no harbor until April 29, when a few naked, thin dark men were seen ashore, armed with stones and boomerangs. Joseph Banks, collecting plants on the dunes, called the place Botany Bay, and later recommended it to the Admiralty as an excellent place to dump convicts after the American Revolution had closed the Atlantic seaboard to transportation of felons. Exploring further northward, the *Endeavour* was grounded on the Great Barrier Reef on the night of June 10. Cook gave up his vessel for lost, but through daring action she was unloaded and finally floated free of the coral pinnacles. Five days later she had made the twenty miles to the mainland, at a harbor now called Cooktown. Two months were needed to repair the vessel so that she could limp through dangerous Endeavour Strait to follow the route of Torres (see No. 14) 164 years earlier. Cook brought his leaky hull to Batavia by October 10. Shipwrights put her into good enough shape to sail by Christmas.

Cook had discovered the cure for scurvy through issuing fresh foods and enforcing hygiene. Ships of his time sailed to the Pacific with double crews, expecting half the men to die of this disease caused by vitamin deficiency, but he was able proudly to write to the Admiralty from Batavia, "I have the satisfaction to say that I have not lost one man by sickness during the whole voyage." But after the fevers of the East Indies and the stresses of the long haul home, only 56 crewmen returned when the *Endeavour* at last anchored below London Bridge on July 13, 1771. Despite many perils, James Cook had charted more than five thousand miles of new coastline on the other side of the world. Although lacking a chronometer to calculate longitude, he had seldom been far off in his reckonings. He had found regions where England might build commonwealths on which the sun would never set.

Cook's second Pacific voyage was designed, despite his earlier achievements, to lay finally the ghost of Terra Australis Incognita. Alexander Dalrymple and some others claimed that Cook still might have missed seeing this Eldorado. This time two ships were sent; but as it turned out, Cook's consort vessel strayed far away and got home a whole year earlier that his ship, the 462-ton *Resolution*, which started with a crew of 112. The 336-ton *Adventure*, with a crew of 82, was commanded by Tobias Furneaux, who had sailed with Wallis. Furneaux was a fair seaman but unadventurous, and the achievement of his ship was hampered by his carelessness in following Cook's anti-scurvy rules.

Banks and his naturalists declined to go on this second voyage, and two Germans, father and son, named Forster, were cranky shipmates. Four chronometers enabled Cook to compute longitude more easily. The two ships sailed from Plymouth on July 13, 1772. After Cape Town, the vessels beat south into the ice pack, and on January 17, 1773, were the first ever to cross the Antarctic Circle. Below the latitude of 67°, Cook could not push farther toward the South Pole. Later crisscrossing of the southern part of the globe proved that there could be no Terra Australis larger than the present shores of the continent of Antarctica—a continent that Cook may have glimpsed through mist.

After a rendezvous in New Zealand, the ships had a happy stay at Tahiti and then visited the regions still known as the Cook Islands. The people of the Tongan group received Cook so well that he called them the Friendly Islanders. On her way back to New Zealand, the *Resolution* had the tip of her mainmast snapped in a storm which separated the ships. Thereafter Cook had to go it alone, as he had in the *Endeavour*. After more summertime ranging of the Antarctic, he rediscovered Easter Island and the Marquesas, and then heading westward saw Nomuka in the Tongas, a small Fijian island, and a group he named the New Hebrides. He also discovered the big island of New Caledonia and its neighboring Isle of Pines. Five weeks later he discovered Norfolk, another pine-clad island. After a stop once more at New Zealand, the *Resolution* headed for home by the roundabout way of Cape Horn, South Georgia, the South Sandwich group, and Cape Town. The ship reached England early in July, 1775, having sailed more than sixty thousand miles in a voyage lasting more than three years—the longest voyage then on record. Not one man had died of scurvy.

Cook was a hero. He might have retired with honors; he was given a sinecure on the governing board of Greenwich Hospital, and his speech to the Royal Society on the prevention of scurvy won the gold Copley Medal for the best paper of the year 1776. He might well have remained at home; but the Pacific called. A third voyage was being fitted out, to repatriate Omai (see No. 24) and to attempt the discovery of a "northwest passage" that would make it possible for ships to sail from Europe directly to the Pacific on a route north of America. Cook agreed to go on his third and last voyage to the Pacific.

Again Cook was to command the *Resolution*, which was worn by three years of battering seas. Her complement was 112 men. Captain of the 295-ton *Discovery*, with a crew of 70, was Charles Clerke, who had been with Cook on the two previous voyages.

The third voyage is the best recorded in eighteenth-century history; no less than twenty-nine logs have survived, in addition to Cook's own. The *Resolution* sailed once more from Plymouth on July 12, 1776, exactly four years after her first departure and one week after the American colonists in Philadelphia proclaimed their Declaration of Independence. But officials of France, America's ally in the war, ordered that the scientific importance of the voyage was so great that Captain Cook should be treated as "the commander of a neutral and allied power".

Cook waited at Cape Town for the arrival of the *Discovery*, delayed by the illness of Captain Clerke. Thereafter, for four years and three months, by supreme seamanship the two vessels were seldom out of sight of each other. At the end of that time, only a few men had died on the *Resolution* from sickness; not one man on the *Discovery* had been lost by scurvy.

The ships put in at Adventure Bay in Van Diemen's Land (Tasmania) to repair the damaged masts of the *Resolution*. They then steered for the old base in New Zealand, sailed through the Cook group to Tonga, and then were at home once more in Tahiti. Omai, the world traveler from the Society group, was put ashore with many gifts at Huahine. Cooked lingered in the warm islands, as if reluctant to battle the storms he knew awaited him in the Arctic. At last he headed northward. At daybreak on January 18, 1778, the ships sighted an island to the northeast and, soon after, another to the north. Next day, another was seen to the northwest. These were Oahu, Kauai, and Niihau, westernmost of the main islands of the Hawaiian group, which Cook named after his patron the Earl of Sandwich.

After trading with the Hawaiians, who spoke a Polynesian dialect similar to that of some Tahitians on board the ships, Cook charted the Oregon coast and then spent almost a year vainly seeking passages back to Europe north of America or Asia. The ships were the first to cross the Arctic Circle from the Pacific side, and penetrated through the ice to 70° 44′ north latitude. James Cook was the first man in recorded history to tread the soil of Europe, Africa, Australia, North and South America, and Asia.

As winter came, the lovely Sandwich Islands beckoned, where the people had greeted Cook as their wandering god Lono. The two "floating islands"—as the ships were called by the Hawaiians

—discovered Maui on November 26, 1778; later the crews glimpsed nearby Molokai, and then for six weeks rounded the large island called Hawaii, seeking harborage from rough weather. A haven was found at Kealakekua Bay on the west shore, where ten thousand Hawaiians greeted the ships and offered supplies.

The full story of Cook's stay in the Hawaiian group and his death during a skirmish on the shore at Kealakekua would make an entire volume. Older than almost any man of his crews, worn by ten years of Pacific discovery, he had accepted the role of a deity and, when the Polynesian custom of "borrowing" ship's property—especially priceless iron—called for the taking of chiefs as hostages, tragedy resulted. James Cook died as he had lived—doing his duty as he saw it, in the course of discovery on a Pacific shore. The remains of his body were given sea burial, with full honors, in the waters of the future American state of Hawaii.

Two centuries after Cook's historic incursion into the Pacific region, readers now have available, with full details, his own writings on the sea journeys of his last decade. Professor J. C. Beaglehole of the Victoria University of Wellington, New Zealand, has completed his four-volume edition of Cook's

The murder of Captain James Cook on St. Valentine's Day, 1779, on the island of Hawaii, resulted from a fatal series of misunderstandings between Englishmen and Hawaiians.

journals—scholarly monuments to a great discoverer and exemplars of interesting and exact editing. The big books are fully illustrated, contain all necessary introductions and apparatus, and are a treasure-house of facts that can be used by generations of authors to come.

Cook's adventures, related in his own words and edited by Professor Beaglehole, comprise four large volumes, one of them in two parts. Volume I is *The Voyage of the "Endeavour", 1768–1771*. Volume II is *The Voyage of the "Resolution" and "Adventure", 1772–1775*. Volume III is *The Voyage of the "Resolution" and "Discovery", 1776–1780*. Volume IV, *Cook's Life and Voyages: Essays and Lists*, has been announced. The *Portfolio* contains 88 reproductions of original charts and views drawn on the three voyages. The Cook logs of voyages are supplemented by excerpts from other members of the ships' companies. Volume I includes those of Robert Molyneux, William Monkhouse, and others. Volume II includes the journal of William Wales and extracts from the journals of Tobias Furneaux, James Burney, Charles Clerke, and Richard Pickersgill. Volume III includes the journals of Surgeons William Anderson and David Samwell and extracts from those of Charles Clerke, James King, James Burney, and others. These volumes edited by Professor Beaglehole are the cornerstone of any library on the Pacific region.

The bibliography on James Cook is voluminous, and only main items can be mentioned here. Ida Emily Leeson and Mary Barrington edited *Bibliography of Captain James Cook, R.N., F.R.S.* (Sydney: Public Library of New South Wales, 1928). W. P. Strauss listed holdings on Cook and other Pacific area explorers in the Mitchell Library of Sydney in *Mitchell Library Quarterly*, XXX (April, 1960), 124–29. Sir Maurice Holmes's *Captain James Cook: a Bibliographical Excursion* (London: F. Edwards, 1952) is a revised and greatly expanded edition of the author's bibliography of 1928. An up-to-date annotated bibliography of James Cook, including references in the Beaglehole volumes and other works since 1952, is badly needed.

Cook himself was not entrusted with the task of reporting to the world the official account of his first voyage. Dr. John Hawkesworth, a literary gentleman adept at ornate rewriting, who never made any voyages himself, compiled a popular work from journals and from papers supplied by Joseph Banks. The three-volume *Account of the Voyages Undertaken by the Order of His Present Majesty for Making Discoveries in the Southern Hemisphere . . .* (London: W. Strahan & T. Cadell, 1773) comprises the voyages of John Byron, Samuel Wallis (see No. 19), Philip Carteret (see No. 20), and Cook's *Endeavour*. The original manuscript of Cook's journal of this first voyage was not published until 1893, under the title of *Captain Cook's Journal During His First Voyage Round the World, 1768–1771* . . . (London: E. Stock, 1893), edited by W. J. L. Wharton.

Cook did prepare the official account of the second voyage, *A Voyage Towards the South Pole and Round the World . . . in Which is Included Captain Furneaux's Narrative of His Proceedings in the "Adventure" During the Separation of the Ships*, 2 vol. (London: Strahan & Cadell, 1777). It was eagerly awaited, and frequently reprinted and translated.

The official account of the third voyage is by James Cook and James King, *Voyage to the Pacific Ocean . . . for Making Discoveries in the Northern Hemisphere* . . . 3 vol. (London: printed by W. & A. Strahan for G. Nicol and T. Cadell, 1784). The first two volumes were written by Cook; after his death on February 14, 1779, the work was continued by his successor in the *Resolution*, James King. This work was also frequently reprinted—often in abridged form—and translated widely.

Among other writings by Cook, the most historic is *A Discourse upon Some Late Improvements of the Means of Preserving the Health of Mariners* . . . (London: Royal Society, 1776), usually included in the account of the second voyage. A quarter of a century later, the British Navy began issuing rations of lime juice to avert scurvy.

Among the various collections of the three voyages are *Voyages of Discovery*, edited by Sir John Barrow (Edinburgh: Black, 1874; in Everyman's Library, London: Dent, 1906; New York, Dutton, 1906) and *The Voyages of Captain James Cook Round the World, Selected from His Journals*, edited by Christopher Lloyd (London: Cresset Press, 1949).

To prevent crew members from forestalling publication of official accounts, the Admiralty requested that all journals be turned in before the conclusion of the voyages. On the first voyage, for example, ten journals were collected by Cook; of these, seven were later reprinted in *Historical Records of New South Wales*, I (Sydney: Government Printer, 1892). Regardless, various men did not turn in their journals or else kept copies, because various volumes by Cook's shipmates were printed. Most important is *The "Endeavour" Journal of Joseph Banks, 1768–1771*, edited by J. C. Beaglehole, 2 vol. (Sydney: Public Library of New South Wales, 1962).

The earliest printed account of the first voyage, published anonymously two months after Cook's return and nearly two years before Hawkesworth's *Account*, is *A Journal of a Voyage Round the World, in His Majesty's Ship "Endeavour", in the Years 1768–1771* . . . (London: Thomas Beckett & P. A. De Hondt, 1771). It has been variously attributed to James Magra or Matra, the American midshipman; to B. Lauragais; and to Hawkesworth himself. *A Journal of a Voyage to the South Seas, in His Majesty's Ship, the "Endeavour"* (London: printed for the editor, 1773), by Sydney Parkinson, who died on January 26, 1771, during the voyage, was edited by his brother Stanfield.

Three unauthorized volumes preceded the official account of the second voyage. *Journal of the "Resolution's" Voyage in 1772, 1773, 1774, and 1775, on Discovery to the Southern Hemisphere* . . . (London: F. Newbery, 1775) appeared surreptitiously and anonymously about eighteen months before Cook's own volumes: it was probably based on the journal of John Marra, one of the gunner's mates. *A Second Voyage Round the World* . . . (London: printed for the editor, 1776) is another surreptitious account, from the journal of one of the officers. John Reinhold Forster, the German naturalist, was originally engaged to write the official record, but after disputes with the Admiralty was forbidden to publish an account. He circumvented this order by attributing the authorship of *Voyage Round the World in His Britannic Majesty's Sloop "Resolution"* . . ., 2 vol. (London: B. White, J. Robson, P. Elmsly, & G. Robinson, 1777) to his son, Johann Georg Adam Forster, who was only seventeen years old when the voyage began. Dismissed by the Admiralty, the senior Forster went to Germany and published an edition of this work in German in Berlin in 1779–1780. He also published a volume of *Observations* made on the voyage (London: G. Robinson, 1778).

Four unofficial volumes anticipated those of Cook and King on the third voyage. A German foremast hand, Heinrich Zimmermann, issued a book at Mannheim in 1781. Two English translations have been made—*Account of the Third Voyage of Captain Cook, 1776–1780*, by U. Tewsley (Wellington: W. A. G. Skinner, 1926) and *Zimmermann's Captain Cook*, by F. W. Howay (Toronto: Ryerson Press, 1930). John Rickman, second lieutenant of the *Discovery*, published *Journal of Captain Cook's Last Voyage to the Pacific Ocean* . . . (London: E. Newbury, 1781). William Ellis, surgeon's second mate, blighted his prospects by publishing *An Authentic Narrative of a Voyage Performed by Captain Cook and Captain Clerke* . . ., 2 vol. (London: printed for G. Robinson, J. Sewell and J. Debrett, 1782). The book by John Ledyard, American corporal of marines, *A Journal of Captain Cook's Last Voyage to the Pacific Ocean* (Hartford, Conn.: Nathaniel Patten, 1783), was based heavily on Rickman. A valuable contribution by a skilled writer, David Samwell, surgeon's mate, is *A Narrative of the Death of Captain Cook* . . . (London: G. G. J. and J. Robinson, 1786), which appeared after the official account.

Biographies have continued to appear since the first one, *The Life of Captain James Cook* (London: G. Nicol, 1788), by Andrew Kippis. It contains abstracts of the three Pacific voyages, draws heavily upon Samwell, and includes biographies of Charles Green the astronomer, John Ledyard, and Captain Charles Clerke. Others include Walter Besant's *Captain Cook* (London and New York: Macmillan, 1890); Arthur Kitson's *Captain James Cook, R.N., F.R.S., the Circumnavigator* (London: J. Murray, 1907); Sir Joseph H. M. Carruthers's *Captain James Cook, R.N.: One Hundred and Fifty Years After* (London: J. Murray, 1930); Rear Admiral John Muir's *Life and Achievements of Captain James Cook, R.N., F.R.S.* (London: Blackie, 1939); Arthur Hugh Carrington's *Life of Captain Cook* (London: Sidgwick & Jackson, 1939); and Christopher Lloyd's *Captain Cook: a Biography* (London: Faber & Faber, 1952). J. M. Gwyther's *First Voyage* (London: Melrose, 1955) has the American title of *Captain Cook and the South Pacific: the Voyage of the "Endeavour"* (Boston: Houghton, Mifflin, 1955). In Roderick Cameron's *The Golden Haze: With Captain Cook in the South Pacific* (London: Weidenfeld & Nicolson, 1964; Cleveland, Ohio: World, 1964), the author deals with

Cook's exploits but throughout the narrative weaves incidents of his own Pacific journey two centuries later. *Captain Cook: the Seaman's Seaman* (London: Hodder & Stoughton, 1967; *Captain James Cook*, New York: Scribner, 1967), by Alan Villiers (see No. 9), the world's foremost living navigator in sail, is especially valuable for light on problems of seamanship faced during the voyages. Two books with many pictures, some in color, are *Captain Cook and the South Pacific*, by Oliver Warner (New York: Harper & Row, 1963) and *The Voyages of Captain Cook*, by Rex and Thea Rienits (London and New York: Hamlyn, 1968). Two small volumes of interest are J. C. Beaglehole's *Captain Cook and Captain Bligh* (Wellington: Victoria University, 1967) and R. A. Skelton's *Captain James Cook After Two Hundred Years* (London: British Museum, 1969).

Except for Geoffrey Blunden's *Charco Harbour* (New York: Vanguard, 1968), good historical novels about James Cook are rare. One is *Lost Eden* by Paul McGinnis (London: Quality Press, 1953; New York, McBride, 1947), whose main character, a sailor, deserts and lives in Hawaii. Perhaps the glamor of the bare facts of James Cook's achievements makes it difficult for the fictionist to improve upon reality.

[23] **GEORGE VANCOUVER.** *Voyage of Discovery to the North Pacific Ocean and Round the World in the Years 1790–1795 . . .* 3 vol. and atlas. London: C. J. and J. Robinson, J. Edwards, 1798.

George Vancouver (1758–1798), whose repute suffered in comparison with the achievements of his fellow explorer James Cook, was nevertheless a highly competent naval officer in the Pacific and charted much of America's northwest coast.

Vancouver entered the British Navy as an able seaman at the age of thirteen and served on board the *Resolution* during Cook's second Pacific voyage. Vancouver was a midshipman on the *Discovery* on Cook's third and last voyage. After passing for the rank of lieutenant, he saw action in the West Indies under Admiral George Rodney. As early as September, 1789, he was appointed to an exploring expedition to the South Seas in a new vessel, also named *Discovery*, which was fitted out under Vancouver's supervision. Departure was delayed by the "Nootka Sound Controversy", but the ship sailed from Falmouth under Vancouver's command on April 1, 1791, supported by the tender *Chatham*.

Vancouver was instructed to handle the return of the furtrading Nootka region "which the Spaniards had seized", and to discover the Northwest Passage. The ships touched at the Cape of Good Hope, surveyed the southwest coast of Australia, explored Dusky Bay in New Zealand, and reached Tahiti at the end of 1791. After diplomatically settling the repossession of Nootka, Vancouver discovered the Gulf of Georgia and circled the large island bearing his name. He spent two years precisely charting and naming the coasts and inlets north of San Francisco. He made three important visits to the Hawaiian Islands and acted as adviser to Kamehameha I, who understood that Britain was offering a protectorate over the archipelago. Vancouver also sought but naturally was unable to find the imaginary group of islands between Hawaii and California which La Pérouse (see No. 26) suggested were those reported by Juan Gaetano, pilot of the Villalobos expedition from Mexico in 1542.

The *Discovery* returned to England by way of Cape Horn, escaping capture by the French during wartime, and arrived in the Thames in October, 1795. Vancouver spent the remainder of his life, in ill health, preparing his journals for publication. He had corrected the proofs of all but the last few pages when he died in May, 1798. The adventures of the *Discovery* and the *Chatham* form a number of exciting episodes in Pacific history, which Vancouver relates in a flowing style.

Edward Heawood, geographical authority, considered Vancouver's survey the most arduous that any navigator had undertaken. Like Cook before him, Vancouver was ordered to find the fabled Northwest Passage across North America, but as one of his biographers wrote: "It is likely that he was prouder of proving the absence of a Northwest Passage within the limits of his survey than he was of the map that resulted from the search." The claims of Britain to the Canadian Northwest were based on the explorations of Cook and especially those of Vancouver—without whose work Canada might not today have any outlet to the Pacific, for the United States claimed the Columbia watershed by virtue of Robert Gray's discovery of that great river.

Biographies of Vancouver include George Stanley Godwin's *Vancouver: a Life* (New York: Appleton, 1931); Roderick L. Haig Haig-Brown's *Captain of the "Discovery"* (London and Toronto: Macmillan, 1956); and Bern Anderson's *Surveyor of the Sea: The Life and Voyages of Captain George Vancouver* (Seattle, Wash.: University of Washington Press, 1960).

[24] **BLAKE CLARK.** *Omai: First Polynesian Ambassador to England.* San Francisco: Colt Press, 1940.

"Omai" was the first South Sea Islander to be taken to England and returned to his home. He went aboard the *Adventure* at Huahiné, in the Society Islands, in 1773 during Captain Cook's second Pacific voyage (see No. 22). He became the pet of London, met Fanny Burney and Samuel Johnson, and was twice painted by Sir Joshua Reynolds. One of the purposes of Cook's fatal third voyage was to repatriate Omai. The returning young Polynesian astonished his friends at Tahiti by strutting in European armor, firing his pistols in the air, and handing out gifts right and left. At his native island the ships' carpenters built a house for him, where a garden and livestock were left for him to attend. Three years later he was dead, and his house had been looted. The only possessions that William Ellis could trace forty years later were a jack-in-the-box and an English Bible with colored engravings.

Blake Clark, born in 1908 at Howell, Tennessee, was an instructor at the University of Hawaii when the Japanese attack came on December 7, 1941, and his book *Remember Pearl Harbor*! (New York: Harper, 1942) was the first of several he wrote about Hawaii. His lively volume on Omai, limited to five hundred copies, unfortunately lacks notes and bibliography. A facsimile reprint was published in 1969 by the University of Hawaii Press, Honolulu. Omai is mentioned in a biography of James Burney by G. E. Manwaring, *My Friend the Admiral* (London: G. Routledge, 1931, 50–52).

Omai, first Polynesian to travel around the world, was returned to his native Society Islands by Captain Cook on his third voyage. Here Omai, in white man's armor and riding a horse, is frightening his friends by shooting his pistol in the air.

[25] GEORGE KEATE. *An Account of the Pelew Islands Situated in the Western Part of the Pacific Ocean, Composed from the Journals of Captain Henry Wilson and Some of His Officers Who, in August, 1783, Were There Shipwrecked in the "Antelope"*. London: G. Nicol, 1788.

The packet *Antelope*, belonging to the Honorable East India Company, during a storm in 1783 struck a rock near one of the "Pelew" or Palau Islands in the Caroline group. Captain Henry Wilson, of the Company's Marines, got all his men safely on shore, and saved many of their supplies. The Englishmen made friends with the Micronesian inhabitants, and observed for the first time the conditions of life in these islands, never previously explored. The castaways built a small vessel from the wreck and all but one man sailed to Macao, finally reaching England in ships of the Company. The Palaus were thus opened to Occidental trade.

Keate's version of the *Antelope* adventure was one of the most popular South Sea narratives of the eighteenth century. Half a dozen British editions appeared in six years. Keate (1729–1797), an English friend of Voltaire, was educated for the law but devoted his talents chiefly to literature; he was described as being inordinately proud of his poems.

When the Englishmen left Palau, "King" Abba Thulle sent with them his son, "Prince" Lee Boo or Liby, to view the blessings of civilization and perhaps bring back some to the islands. This modest young "noble savage" was lionized in London and had higher natural gifts than the more fortunate Omai (see No. 24), but he died of smallpox and was buried in the graveyard of Rotherhithe Parish Church. A little volume about Lee Boo, *The Interesting and Affecting History of a Native Brought to England by Capt. Wilson, to Which is Prefixed a Short Account of Those Islands, with Sketch of the Manners and Customs*, appeared in London in 1789.

A literary sequel to the *Antelope* story is the rare *A Letter to Madan Blanchard* (London: Hogarth Press Letters, No. 1, 1931), by the English novelist E. M. Forster. It is directed—many years too late—to the one crewman who decided to remain on a Micronesian island when all his comrades were leaving, and also gives some information about the young prince's life in London.

Forster cites as a source *A Supplement to the Account of the Pelew Islands; compiled from the Journals of the "Panther" and "Endeavour", Two Vessels Sent by the Honorable East India Company to Those Islands in the Year 1790*, by the Rev. John Pearce Hockin, of Exeter College, Oxford, M.A., (London: printed for Captain Henry Wilson by W. Bulmer, 1803).

[26] JEAN FRANÇOIS DE GALAUP, COMPTE DE LA PÉROUSE. *A Voyage Round the World in the Years 1785, 1786, 1787, and 1788.* 2 vol. Translated from the French. London: John Stockdale, 1798.

King Louis XVI of France decided to send out an exploring expedition in the hope of rivalling Cook and other British discoverers. Two 500-ton armed frigates, *Boussole* and *Astrolabe*, sailed from Brest in August, 1785. Each carried volunteer crews of 218 officers and men. The ships' chart rooms held the best maps available, as well as books on previous voyages. The hold was loaded with supplies and trade goods suitable for a four-year circumnavigation. Commander of the *Astrolabe* was Fleuriot de Langle. Commander of the *Boussole* and head of the expedition was the Comte de la Pérouse, whose title was derived from a little property on his estate in southern France.

The man who was thus challenged to become the French Captain Cook was born in 1741 of a noble family. He became a midshipman in the French Navy in 1756. Made prisoner during the Battle of Quiberon Bay in 1759, he was treated kindly during his only visit to England. He returned to naval service and held a number of commands; the most important was an expedition in 1782 that captured British forts defending Hudson Bay.

The *Boussole* and *Astrolabe* entered the Pacific through the Strait of Le Maire in January, 1786. They touched at Easter Island and the island of Hawaii, and the men were the first foreigners to go ashore on the island of Maui (May 28). They spent four months surveying the California coast, and then sailed for Asia by way of Alaska. In midsummer, entering a dangerous Alaskan bay, the ships were nearly lost and three boats were caught in the breakers, with a loss of twenty-one men, including six officers.

Heading westward, La Pérouse named Necker, an islet in the Hawaiian Chain, and next day the two ships were again almost wrecked, on an uncharted reef still called French Frigate Shoal. They called at the Marianas and the Bashi group before reaching Macao on January 3, 1787. Thence they sailed to the Philippines, where at Cavite they were repaired and supplied.

After exploring Formosa (Taiwan), the coast of Japan, and the Aleutian Chain, the expedition entered the Russian port of Kamchatka in September. There a young officer, later to become Vicomte de Lesseps, who spoke Russian well, was charged with the delivery of the report of the achievements of the expedition up to that date. He delivered his box of papers to the French minister in St. Petersburg after making a journey across Russia and Siberia lasting a full year. These papers were the basis of most of the published accounts on the achievements of the enterprise.

Meanwhile the two ships had visited the Samoan group, where Captain de Langle and eleven of his crew were massacred by the native people of Tutuila when the boats of a watering party were caught on a reef. By way of Tonga and Norfolk Island, La

Fleuriot de Langle, La Pérouse's fellow captain, and eleven of his men were killed by Samoan tribesmen when their boats were stranded on a reef at Tutuila; many others were wounded by clubs and sling stones.

Pérouse headed for Botany Bay, a few miles south of the present Australian metropolis of Sydney.

There, by an amazing chance, he found a British squadron at anchor. It was the famous First Fleet of seven vessels that was to found the continent-wide nation of Australia. Governor Arthur Phillip of the penal colony offered to send the journal of La Pérouse and various letters to the French ambassador in London.

The *Boussole* and *Astrolabe*, loaded with wood and water, put to sea on January 26, 1788, without telling the English where they were bound. Thereafter they disappeared from history for forty years.

Every ship heading for the Pacific was cautioned to seek for traces of the fate of the two frigates and their crews. During the throes of the great French Revolution, nothing was done until, in February, 1791, the National Assembly asked the king to send another expedition to search for La Pérouse and carry on further scientific work in the Pacific. Two 500-ton ships—the *Recherche*, commanded by Rear Admiral Joseph Antoine Bruni d'Entrecasteaux, and the *Espérance*, under Captain Huon de Kermadec—left Brest in September (see Jacques Julien Houton de Labilliardiere, *Voyage in Search of La Pérouse*, 2 vol., translated from the French, London: J. Debrett, 1800). This expedition made many discoveries, yet found no trace of the vanished frigates. The two commanders left their names on various parts of the Pacific map, but both died on the way home and the ships were detained by the Dutch, then at war with the French Republic. Louis XVI was sent to the guillotine, and Napoleon rose to rule Europe. A reward had been offered in 1791 by the French government for any news of the ships of La Pérouse, but thirty-eight years were to pass before any man rose to claim it. That man was Captain Peter Dillon (see No. 43).

Translations of the original three-volume French edition of 1797 were extremely popular in England. A second printing of the Stockdale first publication came out in 1799. Another translation, printed in 3 vol. by J. Johnson, appeared in 1798 after the Stockdale one; a third translation was published in 2 vol. in 1799 by J. Robinson, and is usually the basis for later issues. Aside from these London editions, there was one published in Edinburgh in 1798, with added matter. Thus within two years, British readers had a choice of four different editions of the La Pérouse story, with different engravers used to make plates. An abridgment soon appeared in America (Boston: printed for Joseph Bumstead, 1801).

The condensation of 1839 by F. Valentin, recently translated by Julius S. Gassner, with illustrations and supplements, was published in Honolulu by the University of Hawaii Press and the Friends of the Library of Hawaii in 1969, under the title of *Voyages and Adventures of La Pérouse.*

[27] **WILLIAM BLIGH.** *A Voyage to the South Sea, Undertaken by Command of His Majesty, for the Purpose of Conveying the Bread-Fruit Tree to the West Indies, in His Majesty's Ship the "Bounty"* . . . London: G. Nicol, 1792.

"The volume of literature written concerning the exploits of a naval lieutenant and forty-five men far exceeds the amount written on any other similar voyage," says H. B. Muir in "The Literature of the *Bounty*", in Charles Barrett (ed.), *The Pacific: Ocean of Islands* (Melbourne: Seward, 1950, 87).

The basic book about this most famous of all maritime mutinies is the account by Lieutenant William Bligh, who on April 28, 1789, when his vessel *Bounty* was off the Tongan island of Tofua, was seized in his cabin by Master's Mate Fletcher Christian and others and forced with eighteen loyal crewmen into the ship's launch. Although the mutiny was bloodless, the aftermath was dramatically brutal, and no less than half the crew of the notorious vessel came to violent ends.

Bligh (1754–1817), enrolled on the roster of a British warship at the age of seven, was on duty at sea as a midshipman at sixteen. He passed for lieutenant at the age of twenty-two, and was only twenty-four when, as sailing master under Captain James Cook (see No. 22), he witnessed the murder of his commander at Kealakekua Bay on the island of Hawaii. After marriage and an interlude in the merchant service, Bligh was chosen at the age of thirty-two to command the armed transport *Bounty*. This vessel set sail from England late in 1787 for Tahiti, to load a number of young breadfruit trees to be transplanted in the West Indies as cheap food for slaves on the plantations there.

The ship was greeted by the people of Tahiti on October 25, 1788, but because of delays Bligh had arrived at the wrong time for shipping the young plants. More than five months of exposure to the charms of the "New Cytherea" led to attempted desertions and to bonds between the Tahitians and the seamen, who were at the traditional mercy of a captain with a fiery temper. By a series of grim accidents Christian, who had planned to desert off Tofua in one of the boats, was able to find other disaffected men on deck, to obtain arms, and to seize the ship. He and his supporters probably did not expect Bligh to survive in the overladen, 23-foot launch, but Bligh magnificently guided the boat on a 3,400-mile passage to Timor with the loss of only one man. Bligh there bought a small schooner and continued to England. He was honorably acquitted for the loss of the *Bounty*, and was, moreover, assigned in April, 1791, to command the *Providence* on a second breadfruit voyage; this was successfully accomplished,

Triumph of Fletcher Christian over William Bligh during the mutiny of the *Bounty*. Loyal officers and men have been put overside in the ship's launch. Bligh, still in shirtsleeves, promises punishment of the mutineers, who stand between tubs of breadfruit seedlings and shout "Huzzah for Tahiti!"

but ironically the people of the West Indies disdained adding breadfruit to their limited diet.

Captain Edward Edwards (see No. 28) had been sent from England in November, 1790, to seize any of the *Bounty* mutineers he could find. After his disastrous voyage, ten mutineers were put on trial, and three were executed in October, 1792. Bligh suffered criticism because he was not at the trial, but of course he was away on duty in the *Providence*.

The voyage of the *Providence* resulted in important geographical discoveries, and Bligh continued in the naval service. As commander of the 64-gun *Director* he was involved, among many other captains, in the mutiny of the Nore in 1797, but he helped to settle the grievances of the striking seamen, and was not relieved of his command. He took his ship into the Battle of Camperdown on October 11, 1797, and fought valiantly against the Dutch flagship. His greatest success came when, as captain of H.M.S. *Glatton* at the Battle of Copenhagen on April 2, 1801, he was commended by Lord Nelson. The following month Bligh was made a Fellow of the Royal Society.

Bligh's second deposition by mutineers came when, as fourth governor of the penal colony of New South Wales, charged with putting down corruption by the notorious "Rum Corps", he was arrested early in 1808 by officers of that volunteer regiment, but remained in the colony until April, 1810. His naval rank was restored and he was promptly promoted to rear admiral. At the comfortable age of sixty-four, leaving behind six daughters, William Bligh died peacefully in bed as a British vice admiral.

Publications dealing with the *Bounty* mutiny and its aftermath form a sizeable library. First among these, of course, are Bligh's own writings. Preceding the *Voyage to the South Sea* is his *Narrative of the Mutiny on Board His Majesty's Ship "Bounty"* . . . (London: G. Nicol, 1790; Philadelphia: William Spotswood, 1790), which was reprinted and translated into several languages. As the author says in his "advertisement" to the later *Voyage*, the *Narrative* was published "for the purpose of communicating early information concerning an event which had attracted the public notice: and being drawn up in a hasty manner, it required many corrections". For this and other reasons he prepared the fuller account, which opens with a statement of the plan of the expedition, covers the voyage to the time of the mutiny, describes the cruise of the launch, and ends with his return to England. The tone is quite objective, if we consider his choleric temper and the fact that he was burning with feelings of insult and the need for vindication, as expressed in letters and memorials at the time. The book was reprinted twice in two years, and translated into French and German. An unabridged, illustrated edition of the *Voyage*, entitled *Bligh and the "Bounty"*, was edited by Laurence Irving (London: Methuen, 1936; New York: Dutton, 1936). Another, *Bligh of the "Bounty"*, edited by E. A. Hughes (London: Dent, 1928), contains extracts from the *Voyage* and the *Narrative* in full. Many later editions of the *Voyage* have appeared; the most recent is a facsimile issued by Rare Books (Honolulu: 1967).

Other books by Bligh include *Log of the "Bounty"*, edited by Owen Rutter, 2 vol. (London: Golden Cockerel Press, 1936); *Bligh's Voyage in the "Resource" from Coupang to Batavia, Together with the Log of His Subsequent Passage to England in the Dutch Packet "Vlydt", and His Remarks on Morrison's Journal* . . . (London: Golden Cockerel Press, 1937); *The Voyage of the "Bounty's" Launch as Related in William Bligh's Despatch to the Admiralty and the Journal of John Fryer*, edited by Owen Rutter (London: Golden Cockerel Press, 1934); and *Answer to Certain Assertions Contained in the Appendix to a Pamphlet Entitled "Minutes of the Proceedings of the Court-Martial"* . . . (London: G. Nicol, 1794), written in reply to the defense of the absent Fletcher Christian by his brother Edward.

The standard—and most reliable—biography is *The Life of Vice-Admiral William Bligh, R.N., F.R.S.*, by Dr. George Mackaness (London and Sydney: Angus & Robertson, 1931, 1951; New York: Farrar & Rinehart, 1936), containing a lengthy bibliography. Other lives include Geoffrey Rawson's *Bligh of the "Bounty"* (London: Phillip Allan, 1930; New York: G. R. Gorman, 1937); Owen Rutter's *Turbulent Journey: A Life of William Bligh* (London: Ivor Nicholson & Watson, 1936); and H. S. Montgomerie's *William Bligh of the "Bounty" in Fact and Fable* (London: Williams & Norgate, 1937). A chapter on Bligh in *Rascals in Paradise* by James A. Michener and A. Grove Day

(London: Secker & Warburg, 1957; New York: Random House, 1957) attempts to be objective about a competent royal officer with a penchant for involving himself in courts-martial.

Other books concerning the mutiny include Sir John Barrow's anonymous *The Mutiny and Piratical Seizure of H.M.S. "Bounty"* (London: John Murray, 1831; London: Oxford University Press, 1914), the little book that inspired James Norman Hall (see No. 29). Barrow had access to documents in the British Admiralty. Twentieth-century treatments include *The Court-Martial of the "Bounty" Mutineers*, edited by Owen Rutter in the Notable British Trials series (London: William Hodge, 1931) and Owen Rutter's *The True Story of the Mutiny of the "Bounty"* (London: Newnes, 1936). Selections from various sources, more or less reliable, appear in *The Saga of the "Bounty"*, edited by Irvin Anthony (New York: Putnam, 1935). *A Book of the "Bounty"*, edited by George Mackaness, appeared in Everyman's Library (London: Dent, 1938; New York: Dutton, 1938). A somewhat sensational volume is Alexander McKee's *The Truth About the Mutiny on the "Bounty"* (London: Mayflower Books, 1961; New York: Morrow, 1962). A more reliable, straightforward account is Bengt Danielsson's *What Happened on the "Bounty"* (London: George Allen and Unwin, 1962; New York: Rand McNally, 1962) (see No. 76). Madge Darby's *Who Caused the Mutiny on the "Bounty"?* (Sydney: Angus & Robertson, 1965) argues that Midshipman Edward Young was the secret moving force behind Christian's actions. That controversy concerning the clash of personalities between Bligh and Christian can still be lively is proved by a rebuttal of Madge Darby by Rolf du Rietz (*Studia Bountyana*, I, Uppsala, Sweden: Almqvist & Wiksell, 1965) and her rejoinder (same, II, 1966). The *Providence* voyage is covered by Ida Lee (Mrs. Charles Bruce Marriott) in *Captain Bligh's Second Voyage to the South Sea* (London and New York: Longmans, Green, 1920); the journal of Lieutenant Nathaniel Portlock is included in full.

After the mutineers on the *Bounty* had put their captain and his companions overboard, they shouted "Huzza for Otaheite!" and the ship actually did return to Tahiti. She also made two stops on Tubuai and one probably at Tongatapu, and was the first European ship to sight Rarotonga in the Cook group. Their eight months of wandering ended when they burned the *Bounty* at Pitcairn Island early in 1790.

The occurrences on Pitcairn make a gory narrative of murder and plots. For almost two decades, the surviving fugitives lived on this remote rock before news of their fate reached the outside world. The first visitor to hear their story from the lips of aged John Adams, alias Alexander Smith, sole survivor of the nine mutineers who landed on Pitcairn, was Captain Mayhew Folger of the American whale ship *Topaz* in October, 1808; the account is preserved in Amasa Delano's *A Narrative of Voyages and Travels* (see No. 31). (Folger's discovery came, coincidentally, during the year of the "mutiny" against Bligh in New South Wales.) The next interviews with Adams were reported in 1814 by the captains of two British frigates, Sir Thomas Staines of the *Briton* and Philip Pipon of the *Tagus*, who were seeking out the American raider *Essex* (see No. 37) during the War of 1812. The longest and most detailed extant account based on Adams is found in Captain F. W. Beechey's *Narrative of a Voyage to the Pacific and Beering's Strait*, 2 vol. (London: Henry Colburn and Richard Bentley, 1831); the population of Pitcairn at the time of his visit in 1825 numbered seventy-six. The final account of an Adams interview was recorded by J. A. Moerenhout in *Voyages aux Iles du Grand Océan* (Paris: Arthus Bertrand, 1837). Two accounts by a Tahitian woman named Teehuteatuaonoa or "Jenny", who had been the wife of Isaac Martin on Pitcairn before returning to Tahiti, were taken down at Papeete, translated, and published in 1819 and 1826; a third version appears in Otto von Kotzebue's *A New Voyage* (see No. 37). Walter Brodie in *Pitcairn Island and the Islanders in 1850* (London: Whitaker, 1851) includes a narrative by Arthur, son of Matthew Quintal. Lady Diana Belcher published *The Mutineers of the "Bounty" and Their Descendants on Pitcairn and Norfolk Islands* (London: John Murray, 1870; New York: Harper, 1871); she was Peter Heywood's stepdaughter and owned James Morrison's original *Journal*, and her biased use of this document to exculpate Heywood, a condemned but pardoned mutineer, destroys the value of the book for Dr. George Mackaness, biographer of Bligh. Rosalind Amelia Young, in her *The Mutiny of the "Bounty" and Story of Pitcairn Island* (Oakland, California:

Pacific Press, 1894), gives some details by Eliza, daughter of John Mills, a woman who reached the age of ninety-three.

By 1831 the increase on Pitcairn was so great that the entire population was shipped to Tahiti, but after only five months all but seventeen were back on their beloved home island. Again in 1856 the numbers had increased and all were settled on Norfolk Island near the Coral Sea. Many, however, managed to return to their precious rock Pitcairn.

Accounts are available—more or less reliable—by some of the accused mutineers themselves. Two volumes purportedly by the ringleader, Fletcher Christian—*Letters . . . Containing a Narrative of the Transactions on Board H.M.S. "Bounty"* . . . (London: H. D. Symonds, 1796) and *Voyages and Travels . . . and a Narrative of the Mutiny on Board H.M.S. "Bounty" at Otaheite* . . . (N.P.: H. Lemoine, 1798) are believed by Dr. Mackaness to be clever forgeries. The only first-hand authentic record by a mutineer is the *Journal of James Morrison, Boatswain's Mate of the "Bounty"* (London: Golden Cockerel Press, 1935); Morrison was sentenced to death but pardoned, and re-entered the naval service (see *The Morrison Myth* by H. S. Montgomerie, London: privately printed, 1938). *A Memoir of the Late Captain Peter Heywood* was published by Edward Tagart (London: Effingham Wilson, 1832). The period between the mutiny and the arrival at Pitcairn is well covered by H. E. Maude in "In Search of a Home", Chapter 1 in *Of Islands and Men* (London: Oxford University Press, 1968); Chapter 7, "Tahitian Interlude", documents the first resettlement of the Pitcairn population.

Informative volumes on the Pitcairn story are available. An early account is Thomas Boyles Murray, *Pitcairn: The Island, the People, and the Pastor* (London: Society for Promoting Christian Knowledge, 1853; New York: E. & J. B. Young, 1885). *The Heritage of the "Bounty"* by Harry Shapiro (New York: Doubleday, 1936, 1963) is a highly readable study of human micro-evolution by an ethnologist; the second, softbound edition is revised. Two recent volumes about these British-Polynesian people are Robert B. Nicholson's *The Pitcairners* (Sydney: Angus & Robertson, 1964) and David Silverman's *Pitcairn Island* (Cleveland, Ohio: World, 1967).

Aside from the use made by Nordhoff and Hall and their

predecessors (see No. 29), the *Bounty* story has inspired various literary treatments. Mary Russell Mitford published a long romantic poem in four cantos, *Christiana, the Maid of the South Seas* (London: A. J. Volpy, 1811); in her introduction she hopes that "there may be some gentle readers who will not refuse to a young and timid female the indulgence which they would withhold from an older and more practised offender". The older offender turned out to be George Gordon, Lord Byron. Fletcher Christian, the ideal of Romantic rebellion, was the hero of Byron's poem *The Island, or Christian and His Comrades* (London: Hunt, 1823), which stresses the ideal existence of the seamen at Tahiti and also draws upon the narrative of Will Mariner at Tonga (see No. 35). C. S. Wilkinson in *The Wake of the "Bounty"* (London: Cassell, 1953) makes a case for the theory that Christian soon escaped from Pitcairn (his grave was never found) and returned to England, and that through William Wordsworth, a friend of the Christian family, Samuel Taylor Coleridge was inspired to write *The Rime of the Ancient Mariner*, whose hero is a doomed rebel who voyages in the South Sea and is the only man of the crew to return home. A novel by a Bountyana scholar is Owen Rutter's *Cain's Birthday* (London: Hutchinson, 1930). The patriarch of Pitcairn is the hero of *Adams of the "Bounty"* by Erle Wilson (London: Angus & Robertson, 1959; New York: Criterion, 1959), a novel which attempts to moderate the popular image of Lieutenant Bligh as a bullying monster. A modern French novelist, Robert Merle, in *The Island* (London: Michael Joseph, 1964; New York: St. Martin's Press, 1964), translated by Humphrey Hare, transposes the *Bounty* into a merchant ship and gives the author free rein to invent the sequence of later events.

[28] EDWARD EDWARDS and GEORGE HAMILTON. *Voyage of the "Pandora" Despatched to Arrest the Mutineers of the "Bounty" in the South Seas, 1790–91.* Introduction by Sir Basil Thomson. London: F. Edwards, 1915.

Captain Edward Edwards was sent in August, 1790, in command of H.M.S. *Pandora,* a 24-gun frigate with a crew of 160 men, to round up the *Bounty* mutineers (see No. 27) and return them to justice in England. Two midshipmen of the *Bounty's* launch were aboard who could identify Bligh's former crewmen. The vessel anchored at Matavai Bay on March 23, 1791, and began collecting the men who had remained in Tahiti either because they considered themselves innocent or because they thought they would never be apprehended. Some had built a schooner in which to flee.

The ringleaders had settled on Pitcairn Island more than a year earlier. At Tahiti one man had been murdered by a companion, who was then killed by the natives. The remaining fourteen surrendered or were caught and brought aboard the *Pandora*. Edwards was a more severe commander than Bligh, and his first lieutenant was even harsher. All the *Bounty* men were assumed to be guilty. They were penned like animals in what they came to call "Pandora's Box", an iron-barred roundhouse built on the frigate's deck. They were shackled in irons in this cage, naked and vermin-covered under the tropical sun. Edwards did not trust his crew, fearing that they might also be tempted by the delights of Tahiti. He also feared that the natives, who had formed many bonds with the alleged mutineers, might try an attack.

The *Pandora*, with the little "pirate-built" schooner *Resolution* as a tender under the command of Master's Mate Oliver, left Tahiti on May 8, and cruised separately among several groups, searching for the missing ringleaders but, of course, finding none. Edwards is credited with the discovery of Turéia in the Tuamotus, Nukunono in the Tokelaus, Rotuma, and two small islands east of the Santa Cruz group. His ship passed Vanikoro and sighted smoke rising on shore; had he investigated, he would undoubtedly have solved the mystery of the disappearance of the La Pérouse frigates (see No. 26) and rescued the survivors.

Attempting to find a passage through the Great Barrier Reef, the *Pandora* was wrecked on the night of August 28. For many hours after she struck, Edwards kept the prisoners in their cage, still in chains and guarded by sentinels with orders to fire among them if they moved. After eleven hours, four of the *Bounty* men, still in manacles, perished when the *Pandora* broke up, drowning along with thirty-one of the ship's company.

When the surviving ten prisoners at last reached England, they were put on trial for their lives. Four were acquitted; of the six found guilty, only three were finally executed in Portsmouth Harbor on October 29, 1792—three and a half years after the mutiny had broken out. Captain Edwards, exonerated for the loss of his ship, rose rapidly in the British Navy and became a full admiral in 1810.

The *Pandora* story must by pieced together from a number of sources. The narrative of Edwards himself consists merely of two brief letters, a fifty-page report to the Admiralty from Batavia, and a brief final report from the Cape of Good Hope. These were not published until 1915, and the only previous account was a book by the rollicking, irresponsible surgeon, George Hamilton, *A Voyage Round the World, in His Majesty's Frigate "Pandora"* (Berwick: W. Phorson and London: B. Law & Son, 1793). An interesting retelling of the episode is Geoffrey Rawson's *"Pandora's" Last Voyage* (London: Longmans, Green, 1963).

[29] CHARLES NORDHOFF and JAMES NORMAN HALL. *The "Bounty" Trilogy*. London: Chapman & Hall, 1933, 1935, 1935; Boston: Little, Brown, 1932, 1934, 1934.

"Nordhoff and Hall", the most famous writing team of the twentieth century, come first to the minds of most readers when mention is made of books about the Pacific Islands.

James Norman Hall (1887–1951), a young "woodshed poet", was born in Colfax, Iowa. He went to Grinnell College and did social work in Boston until the outbreak of the European war. In August, 1914, he joined Kitchener's Volunteer Army, "the First Hundred Thousand", and served as a machine gunner for two years. Released from the British Army in 1916, he joined the Lafayette Flying Corps of the French Foreign Legion, and later flew for the United States Air Service. He was downed over Germany with a dud shell in his engine and spent the last six months of the war as a prisoner. In the Lafayette Escadrille he met his future collaborator, Charles Bernard Nordhoff.

Nordhoff (1887–1947), born in London, son of a noted American author and journalist, was brought to the United States when he was three years old. After a boyhood spent chiefly in Philadelphia and California and on a Lower California ranch, he attended Stanford University for one year and later was graduated from Harvard. He worked on a sugar plantation in Mexico and as a businessman in California. He joined the French Foreign Legion in 1916 and, like Hall, became a pilot in the Lafayette Flying Corps.

The two men did not meet, however, until after the end of the war, when they were asked jointly to edit a history of the Corps. Their first meeting did not presage a partnership lasting twenty-eight years. Both had quite different personalities; but the success of their collaboration lay in the reconciliation of opposites. Each brought to their collaborations certain qualities to complement those of the other.

Both had published flying articles in magazines, and both hoped to escape from the post-war "civilized" world. They yielded in 1920 to "a long suppressed desire to sail for the South Pacific Ocean", hoping to earn their incomes from writing. They spent the first year roaming separately through the islands, and then settled down near each other in Tahiti, both taking Polynesian wives who gave them families. Making the South Seas their special literary province, they wrote some of the best contemporary books on this region.

Their attitudes and working methods were strongly in contrast. Hall, dreamy Midwesterner with more than a touch of the poet, was at first the less methodical of the pair, more inclined to lose himself in happy sociability or to embark on a crazy trip from Tahiti to Iceland. Later he became the guiding spirit, and enjoyed mellow older years. Nordhoff, cold aristocrat, at first worked from seven to twelve and provided the controlled craftsmanship that kept the collaborations on the track. Later, when his Tahitian wife invoked the double standard, he went to pieces, left the South Seas, lived "in hell", and dying, presumably of a heart attack, was buried unmourned.

The most enduring collaboration by Nordhoff and Hall is *The "Bounty" Trilogy*, based on the celebrated mutiny against William Bligh (see No. 27). Strangely, this work was written because of a lack of information. Nordhoff would not have agreed to work on *Mutiny on the "Bounty"* had he known that other novels had used this episode in naval history. According to Hall in his last book, *My Island Home*, when he proposed to Nordhoff that they write a novel about this most famous of sea mutinies, Nordhoff replied, "Someone must have written it long since." Hall answered that the only book he had seen was the one by Sir John Barrow that he had picked up in Paris and brought to Tahiti. Still unconvinced, Nordhoff said: "It's incredible that such a tale could have been waiting a century and a half for someone to see its possibilities." But after "the most painstaking researches", the only fiction they could find was a children's book written in 1845 and listed by the Bishop Museum in Honolulu. It was called *Aleck, the Last of the Mutineers* (Boston: B. Perkins, 1854), and centered around John Adams, alias Alexander Smith.

Nordhoff's doubts were justified. Actually, at least four novels had previously been published about the *Bounty* and Pitcairn Island. These were *The Life of Alexander Smith* [John Adams], *One of the Mutineers of H.M.S. "Bounty"* (Boston: S. T. Goss, 1819), by Charles L. Sargeant; *Jack Adams, the Mutineer*, 3 vol. (London: Henry Colburn, 1838), by Capt. Frederick Chamier; *The Lonely Island, or The Refuge of the Mutineers* (London: J. Nisbet, 1880), by R. M. Ballantyne; and *The Mutineer* (London: T. Fisher Unwin, 1898), by another pair of Pacific collaborators, Louis Becke and Walter J. Jeffery (see No. 68). A London reviewer of this last volume, although commending the effort "to revivify an old tragedy", concluded: "But, after all, the history of the mutiny and of Pitcairn is too well known, and is itself of too romantic a colour to give much scope to the novelist." Had Nordhoff realized that the subject was considered very old hat indeed two generations earlier, he and Hall might well have turned their efforts to an entirely different scene.

The collaborators began work on *Mutiny on the "Bounty"* in 1929. Researchers were recruited to comb the archives of the British Museum for material dealing not only with the mutiny but with sea life at the period. Photostatic copies of Bligh's correspondence and of the records of the court martial proceedings were obtained with the permission of the British Admiralty. Copies of the deck plans and rigging of the *Bounty* were secured, and a British naval officer generously proceeded to build an exact model of the vessel. The standard biography of Bligh by Dr. George Mackaness (Sydney and London: Angus & Robertson, 1931) was in print but was not available to the two novelists (later they became friends with this Australian historian and dedicated *Botany Bay* to him). Sources for *Mutiny on the "Bounty"* are listed by the authors in a brief preface to an illustrated volume (New York: Limited Editions Club, 1947).

The exact role of each collaborator in the first volume is not clear. Hall in *My Island Home* was so reticent that Edward Weeks, their editor, felt called upon to add an epilogue stating what he knew of their methods. A less known commentary consists of two letters written by Hall to Dr. Chilson H. Leonard, librarian of Phillips Exeter Academy in New Hampshire on January 5, 1935, and March 10, 1936. In the first of these he says in part:

"You ask how Nordhoff and I collaborated in writing the *Bounty* story. When we had done our preliminary reading, we of course talked the story over, from every possible point of view, and decided what our method of telling it should be. We hoped, at the start, to write a trilogy, but, being by no means sure that there would be enough public interest in the story to justify us in writing three books, we decided to make the first book as complete as possible and tacked on the Epilogue to take care of the Pitcairn side of the tale. We were very glad when we found that we could proceed with the other chapters, for it was a perfect three-part thing.

"When it came to the task of writing, we divided the story into chapters, each of us taking those which most appealed to him. Then, the first draft completed, we exchanged work, each man criticizing and making suggestions before we did our revising. Throughout the trilogy each chapter is largely the work of one or the other of us, although there are certain paragraphs, sentences, and fragments of sentences written in collaboration." In the letter of March 10, Hall remarked: "The large deletions were made, as I remember it, by the publishers . . . [who] thought that readers would be bored by accounts of native customs. We didn't agree with them, but consented to the omissions."

The "Bounty" Trilogy, which also appears under one cover, was originally published in successive volumes. The first is *Mutiny!* (London: Chapman & Hall, 1933). The American title was *Mutiny on the "Bounty"* (Boston: Little, Brown, 1932), and the English title was changed to the American one in the 1936 edition. The book was the result of three years of steady research and writing. The narrator is Roger Byam, who tells the story at the age of seventy-three. Byam is the only invented character in the book; his real-life counterpart was Peter Heywood, whose name for this reason is omitted from the ship's muster. The novel opens at young Byam's country home, where Bligh invites him to sail on the breadfruit voyage to Tahiti, and then shifts to the vessel anchored off Spithead. Thereafter Byam's adventures are followed through the voyage, the fatal six-month delay at Tahiti during which many men formed attachments ashore, the mutiny, and the aftermath—including Byam's trial aboard H.M.S. *Duke* in Portsmouth Harbour and condemnation to death.

The second volume is *Men Against the Sea* (London: Chapman & Hall, 1935; Boston: Little, Brown, 1934), a shorter novel relating Bligh's 3,600-mile voyage to Timor; the narrator is Thomas Ledward, acting surgeon of the *Bounty*.

The concluding volume is *Pitcairn's Island* (London: Chapman & Hall, 1935; Boston: Little, Brown, 1934), which opens with the arrival of the battered *Bounty* at her last resting place at Pitcairn. An omniscient narrator is used for the novel, but many of the later chapters are given in the words of Alexander Smith, sole survivor of the mutinous crew. The exact events on the bloody isle of Pitcairn will probably never be known, but the authors' conjectures may be as good as any. What is true is that fifteen men and twelve women, of two quite different races, landed on one of the most remote islands on the globe. After a decade, although there were many children, only one man and ten women were left; of the sixteen dead, fifteen had come to violent ends.

Aside from their joint editing of *The Lafayette Flying Corps* (Boston: Houghton, Mifflin, 1920) and a book for young people on a similar subject, *Falcons of France* (Boston: Little, Brown, 1929), all but one of the books by "Nordhoff and Hall" deal with the South Seas. They are *Faery Lands of the South Seas* (New York: Harper, 1921), a mixed collection of sketches; *The Hurricane* (London: Chapman & Hall, 1936; Boston: Little, Brown, 1936), based on the terrifying hurricane on Hikeuru Atoll during the pearl-diving season of 1903; *Dark River* (London: Chapman & Hall, 1938; Boston: Little, Brown, 1938), the tragedy of a child theft at Tahiti; *No More Gas* (London: Chapman & Hall,

1940; Boston: Little, Brown, 1940), a humorous novel about the Tuttle family of Tahiti; and *Botany Bay* (London: Chapman & Hall, 1942; Boston: Little Brown, 1941), about a Loyalist in the American Revolution who is sent as a convict from England to Australia. After *The "Bounty" Trilogy* and *The Hurricane*, however, Nordhoff's drive weakened, and the last two books are probably almost altogether the work of Hall. They are *Men Without Country* (Boston: Little, Brown, 1942), about five convicts of French Guiana who escape in a canoe and finally get to England and join the Free French forces in World War II, and *The High Barbaree* (Boston: Little, Brown, 1945), which begins in the Pacific Islands in World War II but trails off into fantasy.

Other books by Nordhoff with South Sea settings are mainly for younger readers. They are *The Pearl Lagoon* (London: Dent, 1926; Boston: Little, Brown, 1924) and *Island Wreck* (London: Methuen, 1929); the American title of the latter is *The Derelict: Further Adventures of Charles Selden and His Native Friends in the South Seas* (Boston: Little, Brown, 1928).

Other books by Hall concerning the Pacific include *On the Stream of Travel* (Boston: Houghton, Mifflin, 1926); *Mid-Pacific* (Boston: Houghton, Mifflin, 1928); *Shipwreck* (London: Chapman & Hall, 1935; the American title is *The Tale of a Shipwreck*, Boston: Houghton Mifflin, 1934), an account of a voyage to Pitcairn in the track of the *Bounty; Under a Thatched Roof* (Boston: Houghton Mifflin, 1942), a collection of essays; *Lost Island* (London: Collins, 1945; Boston: Little, Brown, 1944), a novel about the impact of American forces on a Pacific island in World War II; *The Far Lands* (London: Faber & Faber, 1951; Boston: Little, Brown, 1950), a love story about the remote ancestors of the Tongans; *The Forgotten One and Other True Tales of the South Seas* (Boston: Little, Brown, 1952); and *My Island Home* (Boston: Little, Brown, 1952).

Two motion-picture versions of *Mutiny on the "Bounty"* were widely screened, and several other novels were also filmed—notably *No More Gas*, under the name of "The Tuttles of Tahiti".

A pioneer dual biography is *In Search of Paradise: The Nordhoff-Hall Story* by Paul L. Briand, Jr. (New York: Duell, Sloan & Pearce, 1966). This book, which reveals that the lives of the two men were almost as fascinating as their fiction, has a comprehensive bibliography. The focus of the study is primarily upon Hall, because "Hall, with an eye to posterity, saved everything, leaving behind thousands of documents to build a life from; Nordhoff, unfortunately, with an eye to waste and destruction, saved nothing". Anyone who has enjoyed reading any of the thirty-six books by Nordhoff, Hall, or "Nordhoff and Hall" should read *In Search of Paradise*.

[30] **ERNEST STANLEY DODGE.** *New England and the South Seas*. London: Oxford University Press, 1965; Cambridge, Massachusetts: Harvard University Press, 1965.

The reciprocal influences of two widely separated and highly different cultures—Yankee and Pacific—are here clearly chronicled.

New England and the South Seas is the first book to trace the participation of men and women from New England on this ocean frontier. It is based upon eight lectures covering explorers; whalers; sea-otter, sandalwood, and *bêche-de-mer* hunters; missionaries; politicians; and paradise seekers.

Ernest S. Dodge was born at Trenton, Maine, in 1913. After studying anthropology at Harvard he joined the Peabody Institute at Salem, Massachusetts, in 1937, when the staff numbered only four persons. Working in a growing maritime museum satisfied his interest in the sea and in ethnology, and the resources of the region, including hundreds of old logbooks, were supplemented by visits to the Pacific. Dodge has been director of the Museum since 1950. He is editor of the *American Neptune*, a journal of maritime history, and is a member of many professional societies. People from New England will recognize in his pages the names of many far-wandering families.

[31] **AMASA DELANO.** *A Narrative of Voyages and Travels in the Northern and Southern Hemispheres* . . . Boston: E. G. House, printed for the author, 1817.

Amasa Delano (1763–1823), born in Duxbury, Massachusetts, a relative of Franklin Delano Roosevelt, was a sea officer for much of his life. His volume gives many factual accounts of Pacific voyaging.

According to his book and an appended biographical sketch by an anonymous friend, he was adventurous from an early age. He volunteered for the Colonial Army at twelve, and was accepted when he was fourteen. He first went to sea in 1779 on a privateer; two years later he shipped to the West Indies on a merchantman. At the age of twenty-three he received his first command, a schooner to South America. Impoverished when his ship foundered off Cape Cod in 1787, he failed to recoup his fortunes and sailed as second officer on the privateer *Massachusetts*, the largest ship built in the United States at that time. His *Narrative* begins at this point, in 1790. During the next twenty years he made three round-the-world voyages and "a voyage of survey and discovery in the Pacific Ocean and Oriental islands". He married, but died in obscurity and childless in Boston.

Delano recognized his "want of an early and academic education", and in his book says: "I always seized every possible opportunity during my whole life for the improvement of my mind in the knowledge of useful literature and those sciences that are immediately concerned with the pursuits to which I have been professionally devoted." His journals were edited by "some friends who had the benefit of an academic education", but still retain the flavor of a seaman who records vigilantly, but sometimes ingenuously, many observations on Pacific life.

Delano's account of the fate of the *Bounty* survivors (see No. 27) was the first to reach American readers in book form.

Amasa Delano is best remembered, perhaps as a leading figure in Herman Melville's novella "Benito Cereno" (1855), which was termed by Edward J. O'Brien in 1928, in *The Fifteen Finest Short Stories*, "the noblest short story in American literature". Melville (see No. 51) based his fiction upon Chapter XVIII of Delano's narrative, giving an account of the capture, off the island of Santa María, of the Spanish ship *Tryal*, which had been secretly taken over by its cargo of Negro slaves.

[32] EDMUND FANNING. *Voyages Round the World, with Selected Sketches of Voyages to the South Seas.* New York: Collins & Hannay, 1833.

An active trader and businessman in the early days of American ventures into the South Pacific was Edmund Fanning (1769–1841) of New York. He made several venturesome voyages and later set up a trading company. His first command, at the age of twenty-eight, was the little brig *Betsey*, which sailed from Connecticut in 1797 laden with provisions and such trade goods as ribbons, beads, mirrors, and jackknives. Early in 1798 the ship sighted a herd of three or four hundred thousand seals on Más Afuera, the westermost island of Juan Fernández. By April the *Betsey* was loaded with sealskins, even in the cabins and bunks of the crew, and more than four thousand other skins were left ashore to be collected later. From this island alone, no less than three million skins were taken by sealers in the next twenty years.

On the way to China to sell his skins, Fanning rescued a missionary in the Marquesas, who returned the favor by warning him of a native attack on the ship. On the long run west, an uninhabited island was found on June 11 and named for Fanning. The captain also underwent a supernatural experience that saved his ship from piling up on a reef under full sail. Three times Fanning woke in the night and came on deck and ordered the ship to be slowed. Otherwise the *Betsey* would have crashed among breakers. At Tinian in the Marianas, Fanning rescued a band of castaways who had been wrecked there fifteen months before. His first round-the-world voyage brought him an income of \$120,000 on an \$8,000 investment and inspired many other Americans to seek profits in the South Seas. The United States Exploring Expedition (see No. 49) was approved by Congress partly as a result of Fanning's recommendations.

A second edition of Fanning's book appeared in 1838 under the title of *Voyages to the South Seas. . . .* Three other editions followed. A more easily available reprint is *Voyages and Discoveries in the South Seas* (Salem, Mass.: Marine Research Society Publication No. 6, 1924). No biographical volume on Fanning has appeared, although a brief note is given by Walter M. Teller in *Five Sea Captains: Their Own Accounts of Voyages Under Sail* (New York: Atheneum, 1960).

[33] LOUIS B. WRIGHT and MARY ISABEL FRY.

Puritans in the South Seas. New York: Henry Holt, 1936.

An interest in Herman Melville's comments on missionaries, backed by acquaintance with the beliefs of seventeenth-century Puritans, inspired these collaborators—both at the time on the staff of the Huntington Library, San Marino, California—to write the most readable account of the adventures of the Protestant missionaries who sought to convert the Pacific islanders to their brand of Christianity.

The authors do not claim to write a complete history of Pacific missions. Mainly they offer the story of the London Missionary Society beginning with the voyage of the *Duff* (see No. 34). To round out the picture they include a chapter on the Wesleyan efforts in Tonga and the American Congregationalists in Hawaii, omitting mission labors in New Zealand as sponsored chiefly by the Church of England. They draw upon original missionary accounts rather than hostile criticisms, and give a quite objective but lively picture of these controversial Christianizing activities, without omitting the many ironies that were lost upon the sober-faced zealots whose contributions to South Sea life were not always beneficial.

[34] WILLIAM WILSON. *A Missionary Voyage to the Southern Pacific Ocean, Performed in the Years 1796, 1797, 1798, in the Ship "Duff", Commanded by Captain James Wilson. . . .* London: S. Gosnell for T. Chapman, 1799.

The *Duff* was the first ship sent into the Pacific with the sole intention of converting the people of the islands. The vessel was purchased by the London Missionary Society, founded in 1795 by a group of middle-class, dissenting English Christians whose solemn intention was to transform Polynesians into replicas of pious Britons. The volunteer captain, James Wilson, had survived great adventures in America and India. The company, selected from a host of applicants who yearned to labor at the notorious island of Tahiti, included four ministers and twenty-six men of various trades and crafts. Eighteen of the party were left at Tahiti in March, 1797; later, ten others were deposited at Tongatapu, and one, William Crook, a gentleman's valet, at the Marquesas. These pioneers were unable to adapt themselves to an extended stay, and after about a year of various adventures most of them had to abandon the field; but they had begun an activity which was to be continued until the present day by their sect as well as a number of others.

The voyage aroused great enthusiasm in England and a second expedition set out in 1799; but the *Duff* was captured by a French privateer and the missionaries returned to England after great hardships. Interest in these activities created a wide audience for the narrative of the first voyage, written by the captain's nephew, William Wilson, first mate. His journal, since it was couched in sailorly style at some length, was abridged and put into shape for publication by the Rev. Thomas Haweis, one of the founders of the Society. Because the aims of the missionary chroniclers were different from those of other groups, their observations, as recorded by Wilson, give information on native life and customs that would be overlooked by explorers or traders.

[35] JOHN MARTIN. *An Account of the Natives of the Tonga Islands . . . Compiled and Arranged from the Extensive Communications of Mr. William Mariner, Several Years Resident in Those Islands.* London: J. Murray, 1816.

John Martin (1789–1869), a successful London physician, is best known because he wrote the big volume usually called *Mariner's Tongan Islands.* It was compiled from the keen recollections of an intelligent but somewhat taciturn young man named Will Mariner (1791–1853). As a boy, in 1804, Mariner had sailed from England aboard the *Port-au-Prince* on a privateering and whaling voyage to the Pacific. After two years, in need of repairs, the vessel was anchored at the island of Lifuka when in a sudden attack the Tongans cut off the ship and massacred most of the

Will Mariner, survivor of the massacre of the *Port-au-Prince*, who was adopted by Finau II and became a chief of the Tongan Islands.

crew. The fifteen-year-old Mariner was luckily taken under the protection of the native "king", Finau II, who later adopted him and made him a chief. Will remained in friendly captivity for four years, from 1806 to 1810, when he escaped on a passing ship and eventually returned to London.

A second printing of Martin's book appeared in 1817 with additions, and a third edition in 1827. The volume not only narrates Mariner's remarkable adventures but also provides a wealth of anthropological information on the Tongan people, for Mariner had mastered their language thoroughly and had a highly accurate memory.

Mariner's recollections can be checked against a little-known volume, *An Authentic Narrative of Four Years' Residence at Tongataboo* . . . (London: Hatchard, 1810), anonymously published by George Vason or Veeson of Nottingham. This author landed at Tonga in 1797 from the *Duff* (see No. 34) as a missionary, but backslid and intermarried with the natives, with whom he lived for two years. He gives a well-written account of Tahiti at this period as well, and describes civil war in Tonga and the murder of three missionaries of the London Missionary Society.

A highly readable biography is *Will Mariner* (London: Faber & Faber, 1936; Boston: Houghton, Mifflin, 1937), by Vice Admiral B. T. Somerville. Mariner's story is more briefly retold in *Rascals in Paradise* (London: Secker & Warburg, 1957; New York: Random House, 1957), Chapter IX, by James A. Michener and A. Grove Day. Mariner is also the main character in Robert D. FitzGerald's *Between Two Tides. Tide* (Sydney: Angus & Robertson, 1952), an epic poem by a celebrated Australian poet who spent five years in Fiji. For dramatic purposes, FitzGerald combines two historical chiefs of Tonga, Finau I and Finau II, into one character, but remains true to the spirit of Mariner's odyssey.

[36] DAVID PORTER. *Journal of a Cruise Made to the Pacific Ocean. . . .* Philadelphia: Bradford & Inskeep, 1815.

David Porter (1780–1843), most celebrated son of a noted American naval family, had his baptism of fire at the age of sixteen in an encounter with a British man-of-war, and later fought the French, the pirates of Tripoli, and the British in the Atlantic in the War of 1812 before rounding Cape Horn and entering the Pacific early in 1813. Porter, first naval commander to show American colors in that ocean, well fulfilled his mission to protect his own whale ships and capture British vessels. His cruise of more than a year away from home waters, supplying his needs from captured ships, was unprecedented in United States naval history. For a time he made his base in the Galápagos Islands and later took possession of Nuku Hiva in the southern Marquesas group, where he set up Fort Madison and admitted the Polynesian inhabitants into "the great American family". Seeking the enemy off South America, he was blockaded at Valparaiso and on March 28, 1813, having escaped from the harbor, his vessel was hit by a disabling squall. He fought the British ships *Phoebe* and *Cherub* until, having lost 155 men out of 225, he was forced to surrender. Paroled, he was still fighting the British on the Potomac in September, 1814.

An abridgment of Porter's journal is entitled *A Voyage to the South Seas in the Years 1812, 1813, and 1814 . . . in the Frigate "Essex"* (London: Sir. R. Phillips, 1823). The standard biography is by his son, David Dixon Porter, *Memoir of Commodore David Porter, of the United States Navy* (Albany, New York: J. Munsell, 1875). A recent retelling is *The Odyssey of the "Essex"* (New York: McKay, 1969), by Frank Donovan.

[37] **OTTO VON KOTZEBUE.** *A Voyage of Discovery into the South Sea and Beering's Straits, for the Purpose of Exploring a North-East Passage* . . . Translated from the German by H. E. Lloyd. 3 vol. London: Longman, Hurst, Rees, Orme, & Brown, 1821.

Otto von Kotzebue (1787–1846), a Baltic German and Russian subject, devoted the best years of his life to service in the Russian Imperial Navy, which at that time was expanding into the Pacific. He was the son of the prolific German playwright August von Kotzebue. At the age of seventeen Otto volunteered to sail with his uncle, Adam Johann von Krusenstern, on a circumnavigation in the ship *Nadeshda*. An account of this voyage was published in English as *Voyage Round the World* . . . translated from the German by R. B. Hoppner, 2 vol. in 1 (London: printed by C. Roworth for J. Murray, 1813). Krusenstern was accompanied by the *Neva*, whose captain, Urey Lisiansky, translated his own account into English, *A Voyage Round the World* . . . (London: printed for J. Booth, 1814). Otto first visited such regions as Hawaii and the Marquesas on this voyage.

A youthful but seasoned officer, in command of his own ship, the *Rurik*, Von Kotzebue explored the Pacific, the west coast of America, Alaska, and Siberia from 1815 to 1818. The German original of his *Voyage of Discovery* appeared in three volumes at Weimar in 1821, and the English translation came out the same year.

Von Kotzebue was commissioned in 1823 by Czar Alexander to make yet another voyage into the Pacific, in command of the ship *Predpiatie*. The English version of the two-volume German account (Weimar and St. Petersburg, 1830) is entitled *A New*

The scene on the island of Hawaii on November 24, 1816, when Captain von Kotzebue and his "gentlemen" interviewed King Kamehameha I and his court. The king is wrapped in a black cloak of bark cloth. To his left sit Kotzebue and three scientists, with Choris, the artist, at the end of the row.

Voyage Round the World . . . (London: H. Colburn and R. Bentley, 1830). This later expedition, on its way around the globe, visited such Pacific islands and groups as Tahiti, the Tuamotus, Samoa, the Marshalls, the Philippines, and Hawaii.

Otto von Kotzebue shared the literary gifts of his father, and is the most graphic and quotable of all the Russian explorers in the Pacific (between 1803 and 1849, there were thirty-six Russian voyages round the world, most of them following the pioneer track of Krusenstern). During the *Rurik* voyage, Kotzebue's staff included three "scientific gentlemen": Adelbert von Chamisso, botanist and poet, who wrote in German a two-volume account of the voyage; Johann Friedrich Eschscholtz, naturalist who gave his name to the California state flower, the golden poppy, and to the atoll of Bikini; and young Louis Choris, artist whose lovely sketches illustrate the official account of the *Rurik* adventure and who published two books in French with pictures of world scenes.

[38] JOHN WILLIAMS. *A Narrative of Missionary Enterprises in the South Sea Islands.* London: John Snow, 1837. New York: Appleton, 1837.

John Williams (1796–1839), "the martyr of Eromanga", was the ablest missionary to the Polynesian people, and his book was the most widely read of all contemporary missionary accounts.

Born in Middlesex, Williams obtained a commercial education and was apprenticed to a London ironmonger. At the age of twenty-one he was accepted by the London Missionary Society and sent to the island of Eimeo (Mooréa), near Tahiti. Restless, zealous, and resourceful, he moved from island to island in central Polynesia, preaching in the native languages and teaching the natives how to use tools and to raise sugar and tobacco, products that could be sold in New South Wales. From local materials,

Missionary John Williams preaching under a tree during one of his tours of the islands for the London Society.

almost without iron, he built a 60-foot vessel, named *The Messenger of Peace*, and in it sailed to many islands, establishing stations and leaving trained native missionaries to continue the work of conversion.

He visited England in 1834, where he aroused a strong interest in the missions and raised money to buy and fit out a new, larger vessel. In this ship, the *Camden*, he returned to the Pacific and soon began to extend his field of labor to the savage New Hebrides group. Having landed at Dillon's Bay, on the island of Eromanga, he was trying to make friends with the natives when they suddenly turned on him and clubbed him to death. The book published two years previously was a best seller in its time and is highly readable today.

[39] **MARNIE BASSETT.** *Realms and Islands: The World Voyage of Rose de Freycinet in the Corvette "Uranie", 1817–1820.* London: Oxford University Press, 1962.

This story of an exciting voyage around the world, told from the point of view of the French commander's wife, who was the only woman aboard, is both scholarly and literary.

Louis Claude Desaulces de Freycinet (1779–1842) was one of four brothers in the French service. He was assigned in 1800 to an expedition sent out by Napoleon to explore Australian waters; two ships, *Géographe* and *Naturaliste*, were commanded by Nicolas Baudin. After Baudin's death on the voyage it devolved upon Louis de Freycinet to edit the maps and reports.

De Freycinet was made commander of another expedition, sent out by the Bourbon king in 1817. Dressed in man's clothing—blue trousers and a long blue coat—Rose Marie Pinon, the young wife of De Freycinet, joined the *Uranie* at Toulon and sailed on September 17, 1817, the only woman among a naval crew of 120 men. Rose, married in 1814, aged nearly twenty, defied regulations to sail with her explorer husband. She was brave but not brazen, and endured hardships because she could not part with a companion to whom she had been married for little more than three years. Louis was charged to carry on investigations in geography, magnetism, meteorology, ethnology, and other sciences. Rose faithfully aided him in housekeeping duties aboard and in offering consolation during the voyage.

The *Uranie* rounded the Cape of Good Hope, called at the Île de France (Mauritius), and after stops at Timor and New Guinea spent three months in the Marianas group in Micronesia. De Freycinet was one of the first French voyagers to visit the Hawaiian Islands, when the *Uranie* stopped at Oahu and Maui in August, 1819. On the way to Port Jackson in Australia, the commander gave to a small, uninhabited coral island to the east of Samoa the name of Rose Atoll, after his wife. It still bears that name on the map. De Freycinet was not aware that Jacob Roggeveen had discovered this islet on January 13, 1722, and named it Vayle Eyland.

After provisioning at Sydney, the *Uranie* went to Tierra del Fuego to continue scientific investigations. The vessel weathered a furious hurricane but was wrecked on a rock in French Bay in the Falkland Islands. All the crew were saved. Domestic details are given by Rose even when camped on a frozen, desolate isle. Finally De Freycinet was able to purchase an American vessel on April 17, 1820, and, renaming it the *Physicienne*, took this relief ship to Montevideo. The De Freycinets returned to France on November 13, 1820, after an absence of more than three adventurous years. A woman's voyage around the world on an exploring ship was ended.

Rose de Freycinet died at the age of thirty-seven when cholera struck Paris in 1832. As her companion Jacques Arago, the artist on the *Uranie*, wrote: "Alas! what storms had not achieved, nor the most dangerous diseases of pestilential climates, cholera accomplished in Paris, and the poor traveler, the active woman, the devoted wife, the amiable and charitable lady, left this world that she had traversed from end to end."

Lady Bassett's book is based not only on many printed sources but upon an original journal kept by Rose de Freycinet; extracts are frequently quoted in English. The author indefatigably searched for her material in various parts of the world. She drew particularly upon the illustrated volume by Arago, in the form of a series of letters to a friend (*Narrative of a Voyage Around the World* . . . translated from the French, London: Treuttel & Wurtz, Treuttel, jun. & Richter, 1823).

Lady Bassett, born Flora Marjorie Masson in 1889, is the wife of Sir Walter Bassett of Melbourne. Her other books include *The Hentys* (Melbourne: Oxford University Press, 1954), about a pioneer family on the southern coast of Australia, and *Behind the Picture: H.M.S. Rattlesnake's Australia–New Guinea Cruise, 1846 to 1850* (Melbourne: Oxford University Press, 1966), during which T. H. Huxley was medical officer (see No. 54).

[40] **WILLIAM ELLIS.** *Polynesian Researches During a Residence of Nearly Eight Years in the Society and Sandwich Islands.* 2 vol. London: Peter Jackson, Late Fisher, Son, & Co., 1829.

Born in London of a poor family, William Ellis (1794–1872) was a gardener before he answered a call to become a member of the London Missionary Society. He was trained and in 1815 ordained for service. He labored first in South Africa and then was sent, with his wife and baby, to the South Pacific, arriving in 1817. There King Pomaré II had become a convert, and the idol Oro overthrown. Ellis spent five years in the Society group, at Tahiti, Eimeo (Mooréa), and Huahine. He was practical as well as zealous, and was the pioneer printer in the South Seas, when a press was set up in 1817.

Ellis's career was changed by the arrival of a deputation from London, headed by the Reverend Daniel Tyerman (1773–1828) and George Bennet. Their account, *Journal of Voyages and Travels . . .* compiled from original documents by James Montgomery, 2 vol. (London: F. Westley and A. H. Davis, 1831; "revised by an American editor", 3 vol., Boston: Crocker and Brewster; and New York: J. Leavitt, 1832), draws heavily upon Ellis's *Polynesian Researches.*

Captain George Vancouver, during one of his visits to Hawaii between 1792 and 1794, had promised King Kamehameha that he would send him a ship. This vessel, the *Prince Regent*, a 70-ton schooner built in Australia, arrived at Tahiti in company with the 61-ton sloop *Mermaid*, and Captain Kent offered passage for a group of missionaries. Ellis, Tyerman, Bennet and two Tahitian Christians—Auna and his wife—sailed in the *Mermaid*, reaching Hawaii on March 28 1822.

After a visit with the American Congregationalist missionaries who had spent barely two years in the "Sandwich Islands", Tyerman and Bennet sailed for the Marquesas, where the tattooed cannibals, since the time of William Crook of the *Duff* (see No. 34), had not received the consolations of Methodism. Ellis remained in Hawaii for a time. His knowledge of the Tahitian language enabled him to learn Hawaiian quickly, and he was the first person to preach a sermon in the latter tongue. He also helped to reduce Hawaiian to a roman alphabet and begin printing in Honolulu.

The American missionaries invited Ellis to work with them permanently. He agreed, and after returning to Huahine to bring his family north, began his labors in 1823. At that time no mission stations had been opened on Hawaii, the largest and most populous island of the group. Ellis was a member of a party sent to Hawaii to choose suitable sites. He began in June a two-month trip around the island. This group were the first white men to ascend the active volcano of Kilauea. When Ellis returned to England a few years later because of his wife's health, he published his *Narrative of a Tour Through Hawaii* (London: printed for the author by H. Fisher, Son, and P. Jackson, 1826; Boston: Crocker & Brewster; and New York: J. P. Haven, 1825). This valuable account formed Part IV of his *Polynesian Researches*.

Ellis in later life served as chief foreign secretary of the London Missionary Society, and made several visits to Madagascar; he wrote a history of that island which appeared in two volumes in 1838. Other works include *A Defense of the Missions in the South Seas* (1827), *A Vindication of the South Seas Mission* (1831), and *The History of the London Missionary Society* (1844). His second wife, whom he married in 1837, was likewise active as a writer and worker for temperance and charity. Nearing the age of eighty, having survived primitive conditions in foreign lands, William Ellis the world traveler died of a chill caught in an English railway carriage.

Ellis's education was that of a British Christian, but his descriptions of the South Seas could not help but verge on the romantic, and aroused much interest among people outside mission circles. Robert Southey, reviewing *Polynesian Researches* in the *Quarterly Review*, remarked: "A more interesting book we have never perused." The work was used as source material by Herman Melville (see No. 51) and other writers. As John Fisher notes: "His *Polynesian Researches*, and particularly the first volume, is a great quarry into which generations of scholars have dug for information; everything is there—scenery and fruits and flowers, fish and birds and insects, histories and legends and traditions of a dying race; temples and idols, weapons and canoes, fishermen with their nets, and young men racing; bloodthirsty ways of war and drums booming for human sacrifice and girls putting flowers in their hair. There was much a good Christian must hate, and much he could never hope to understand, but Ellis hated less, and tried harder to understand than most of his companions." (*The Midmost Waters*, London: Naldrett Press, 1952, 17).

Ellis rightly remarks in his Preface regarding the Polynesians: "All their uses of antiquity having been entirely superseded by the new order of things that has followed the subversion of their former system, the knowledge of but few of them is retained by the majority of the inhabitants, while the rising generation is growing up in total ignorance of all that distinguished their ancestors from themselves. The present, therefore, seems to be the only time in which a variety of facts, connected with the former state of the inhabitants, can be secured." His work covers not only native lore but the progress of the missions in Polynesia during thirty years, as well as remarks on the native governments and foreign intrusions. Ellis during his ten-year absence from England made copious notes and kept a daily journal that could form the basis of his volumes.

Part I, "Polynesia", opens with geographical and historical data, continues with information on fauna and flora, and fills the remaining pages with descriptions of the inhabitants and their customs and beliefs.

Part II, "Society Islands", deals with this group, especially Tahiti. It shows the changes in the traditional culture of the islands during the early nineteenth century under the impact of Occidental ideas, the conversion of King Pomaré II and his rise to dominance, the preaching against human sacrifice and infanticide, and the introduction of a written language and a printing press. The volume is virtually a history of Tahiti from the arrival of the *Duff* in 1797 until Ellis's departure in 1822.

Part III, "Society Islands, Tubuai Islands, and New Zealand", narrates missionary endeavors in these regions and gives much miscellaneous history and lore still valuable to anyone interested in the South Seas as viewed more than a century and a half ago.

Part IV, "Hawaii", consists of an introductory chapter and a brief history of the missionary effort in the islands up to 1822; the remainder of the book is the *Narrative of a Tour Through Hawaii*, first published separately in London in 1826.

Polynesian Researches has gone through a number of reprintings. The most recent facsimile of the second edition is in four volumes, Rutland, Vermont, and Tokyo: Charles E. Tuttle, 1969.

[41] **WILLIAM LAY and CYRUS HUSSEY.** *A Narrative of the Mutiny on Board the Ship "Globe" of Nantucket, in the Pacific Ocean, January, 1824* . . . New London, Conn.: printed for the authors, 1828.

The most gory mutiny in Pacific history broke out on the whale ship *Globe* early in 1824, led by the young harpooner Samuel Comstock, when the ship was near Fanning Island. The story of the destruction of the four officers at sea, the attempt to conquer the Marshallese natives of Mili Atoll, the murder of Comstock, the escape of some of the crew on the shorthanded voyage of the *Globe* to the South American coast, and the amazing rescue of the two young sailors Lay and Hussey is told in this brief account by these two survivors. The story of the rescue is also narrated by Lieutenant Hiram Paulding (see No. 43).

The *Globe* story has been retold in *Rascals in Paradise* by James A. Michener and A. Grove Day (London: Secker & Warburg, 1957; New York: Random House, 1957), Chapter I. It is also the basis for a novel by Edouard Stackpole, *Mutiny at Midnight* (New York: William Morrow, 1939). Another is *Captain Marooner* (New York: Thomas Y. Crowell, 1952) by Louis B. Davidson and Eddie Doherty. A reprint of the Lay and Hussey book appears as *Mutiny on Board the Whaleship "Globe"* (New York: Corinth Books, 1963), with an introduction by Edouard Stackpole.

Murder of Samuel Comstock on the atoll of Mili by his mutinous shipmates.

[42] **HIRAM PAULDING.** *Journal of a Cruise of the United States Schooner "Dolphin" . . . in Pursuit of the Mutineers of the Whale Ship "Globe"*. New York: G. & C. & H. Carvill, 1831.

The *Dolphin* was assigned in 1825 to sail to the "Mulgrave Range" or Mili Atoll in the Marshall group to apprehend the surviving mutineers of the *Globe* (see No. 41). Commanded by the legend-making "Mad Jack" Percival, this fast war vessel visited the Galápagos Islands, the Marquesas, and the southern Gilberts, and reached Mili on November 19. First Lieutenant Paulding is modest in telling of his part in the rescue of William Lay, an episode which provided the key to the sequel to Comstock's mutiny. A midshipman in the launch said that "the boldest act he ever witnessed" was Paulding's singlehanded seizure of Lay on the beach in the face of an armed mob of several hundred Marshallese warriors. As a result, Cyrus Hussey was also rescued from his native masters.

After visiting some other islands in the Marshall group the *Dolphin* touched at several in the northwestern Hawaiian Chain and then refitted at Honolulu (which Paulding spells "Onavoora"). Percival's schooner was the first American naval vessel to stop at the future Fiftieth State. Soon "Mad Jack" stirred up animosity between his seamen, allied with whalers in port, and the Hawaiian rulers, guided by the advice of the "First Company" of New England missionaries, who had landed in the islands in 1820. An edict refusing to permit Hawaiian women to visit aboard ships in the harbor was the cause of the attack on the home of the "prime minister", Kalanimoku, on Sunday, February 26. Paulding passes over this incident in a paragraph, but on his return to America, Captain Percival faced a court-martial for inciting the riot. He was acquitted because he had also quelled the disturbance after it had started.

After four months at Honolulu, the *Dolphin* passed through the Tubuai or Austral group, touched at Rapa, and anchored on July 23, 1826, at Valparaiso.

A reprint of Paulding's lively account of the cruise is now available (London: C. Hurst, 1970; Honolulu: University of Hawaii Press, 1970), with a lengthy foreword by A. Grove Day.

[43] PETER DILLON. *Narrative and Successful Result of a Voyage in the South Seas Performed by Order of the Government of British India, to Ascertain the Actual Fate of La Pérouse's Expedition.* London: Hurst, Chance, 1829.

The account of the solution to the disappearance in 1788 of the two French frigates *Boussole* and *Astrolabe* commanded by the Comte de la Pérouse (see No. 26), given by the man who ended this forty-year-old mystery, is a sea classic.

Peter Dillon was an Irish sailor born around 1785, poor and with little formal education. He towered six feet four inches and had a flaming mop of red hair. He talked in a thick brogue, and when angered would lash out with a sharp tongue, fists, or any object within reach. Peter was a canny trader, however, and respected the native people of the South Seas. His study of their languages and lore helped him to success as a seaman and maritime detective.

As third officer of the ship *Hunter* of Calcutta, Dillon was helping to load sandalwood in 1813 off the east coast of the Fijian island of Viti Levu. After six months had passed and the ship was still short of two-thirds of its cargo of precious wood, the captain sent out a force to punish the Melanesians who had

Peter Dillon, who was destined to solve the mystery of the disappearance of the frigates of La Pérouse, besieged with two companions on a rock off Fiji in 1813 by cannibals who sought to kill them before they could escape to their ship.

failed to keep their promises. The shore party was ambushed, and finally only Dillon and two others—William Wilson and Martin Buchert or Bushart, both expert shots—were left, defending themselves on a tall rock. During a parley, with several thousand howling cannibals cutting up their victims—including Charles Savage—before his eyes, Dillon put his musket to the head of a native priest and marched him through the crowd to one of the ship's boats. This exploit made Peter known among the islands for incredible bravery.

Thirteen years passed, during which Dillon married, obtained his own commands, and continued to study Pacific history, especially the disappearance of the La Pérouse frigates. As owner and captain of the *St. Patrick*, an old vessel under Chilean registry, he stopped on May 5, 1826, at the island of Tikopia on the outskirts of the Santa Cruz group, where in 1813 he had put ashore Martin Bushart and a lascar named Joe. Joe swapped with the ship's armorer, for a few tin fishhooks, an old silver sword guard. Young George Bayly, third mate, showed it to Dillon. On it were engraved three cyphers; the third of these, under a magnifying glass, showed the letter "J.F.G.P."—Jean François Galaup de la Pérouse! Bushart volunteered that he had seen on Tikopia a number of old articles from Europe, which had been obtained by barter with the natives of an island two days' sail to leeward called "Mannicolo". Joe the lascar had once visited there and had seen two Frenchmen belonging to two ships wrecked when these old men had been boys.

Dillon at once headed the *St. Patrick* for this island, today called Vanicoro. When only six or seven miles offshore, he was becalmed. He was in sight of what he was sure was the key to the mystery. But his vessel was taking twenty inches of water an hour and the crew was near starvation. Captain Dillon reluctantly turned about and headed for India, determined to return as soon as possible and rescue the French survivors.

The odyssey of Dillon in his attempt to return to Vanikoro is narrated in full in his book in his own words (since he could neither read nor write, the volume was taken down from his dictation). One drawback after another, including charges against him of insanity and a stretch of imprisonment in Tasmania, hampered his efforts to return, in command of the British ship *Research.* He feared he would be anticipated by a French vessel, another *Astrolabe*, commanded by Jules Sebastien César Dumont d'Urville, sent out to solve the La Pérouse mystery. The conclusive proof of the wrecking of the two ships off Vanikoro is given in Dillon's book, although the two French survivors were never found. Dumont d'Urville, exploring the site six months later, confirmed Dillon's discovery. In Paris on February 22, 1829, the wild Irish seaman was granted by Charles X the reward of ten thousand francs and an annuity of four thousand. On the same day he was created a Chevalier of the Royal Order of the Legion of Honor.

Writings supplementing the story of the missing French frigates are: Dumont d'Urville, *Voyage de la Corvette "L'Astrolabe"*, Paris: S. Tastu, 1830–34); George Bayly, *Sea Life Sixty Years Ago* (New York: Harper, 1886); James W. Davidson, "Peter Dillon and the South Seas", *History Today*, VI (May, 1956), 307–17; and A. Grove Day, *Adventurers of the Pacific* (New York: Meredith Press, 1969), Chapter 6.

[44] JAMES F. O'CONNELL. *A Residence of Eleven Years in New Holland and the Caroline Islands; Being the Adventures of James F. O'Connell.* Edited from his verbal narration [by H. H. W.]. Boston: B. B. Mussey, 1836.

O'Connell's description is the first extensive ethnographic account of the island of Ponape in the Caroline group. His book is a fascinating if frequently unreliable story of his adventures in the Pacific and his subsequent career as the first "tattooed man" to make the rounds of American circuses and carnivals. Part of his act was to relate his hardships and perform the Irish jig that was supposed to have inclined the natives to spare his life when he was cast away on Ponape.

Wrecked on Ponape, O'Connell saves his life and those of his shipmates by doing a lively jig for the natives.

James F. O'Connell (1808–1854?), born in Dublin of a circus family, went to Australia as a cabin boy (or perhaps a convict) and after six years somehow made his way to Ponape; the story that he was a member of the crew of the *John Bull*, six of whom reached the island after four days in an open boat, is probably untrue. The young man was adopted by a native chief, became a chief himself, married his patron's daughter, had two children, and underwent tattooing in the native style (a painful procedure that enabled him to earn his living as a showman after he was taken off Ponape in November, 1833). At least four pamphlets, condensed from his book, were hawked at circuses at which O'Connell performed in the United States after 1835.

Several authorities have accepted the Irish adventurer's accounts of native life as quite authentic. "But some of O'Connell's information is so patently and flagrantly wrong that one wonders whether we are dealing with a pathological liar", is the judgment of Dr. Saul H. Riesenberg, Chairman of the Department of Anthropology at the Smithsonian Institution ("The Tattooed Irishman", *Smithsonian Journal of History*, III, Spring, 1968, 1–18). Dr. Riesenberg analyzes O'Connell's book and has collected many facts about his life that differ from that account. The *Residence* will remain, however, as an entertaining story of beachcomber life.

[45] **TA'UNGA.** *The Works of Ta'unga: Records of a Polynesian Traveller in the South Seas, 1833–1896.* Translated by R. G. and Marjorie Crocombe, with annotations by Jean Guiart, Niel Gunson, and Dorothy Shineberg. Foreword by H. E. Maude. Pacific History Series: No. 2. Canberra: Australian National University Press, 1968; Honolulu: University of Hawaii Press, 1968; London: C. Hurst, 1968.

A Polynesian missionary in the islands of Melanesia and western Polynesia in the last century put down in his own language, over a period of sixty years, his thoughts concerning "what I saw with my eyes, heard with my ears, felt with my hands".

Ta'unga, born on the island of Rarotonga in the Cook group about 1818, learned to read and write Polynesian at a school of the London Missionary Society, and spent his long life spreading its gospel. He was almost certainly the first literate man to spend some time in New Caledonia, which he reached soon after sandalwood had been discovered on the neighboring Isle of Pines. He also labored in the Loyalty Islands and Samoa. His arrival in Melanesia as an emissary of Methodism coincided with the arrival of the rapacious emissaries of trade. Ta'unga wrote of massacres, epidemics, and threats to Christian teachers and followers. He also reported, as a follower of Jesus, concerning native customs dealing with marriage, crops, warfare, and cannibalism, as well as attitudes toward the invading white men.

Thirty of Ta'unga's manuscripts, written between 1833 and 1896, have been listed. Many have here been translated and annotated. Majorie Crocombe, herself born a Rarotongan, says: "In translating we have tried as far as possible to preserve Ta'unga's own style." This book is the first to be published containing the thoughts of a Pacific islander writing about any region other than his own. The unique experiences of a Polynesian missionary among South Sea people has never been better voiced.

[46] **OWEN CHASE.** *Narrative of the Most Extraordinary and Distressing Shipwreck of the Whale-Ship "Essex" of Nantucket. . . .* New York: W. B. Gilley, 1821.

"My God, Mr. Chase, what is the matter?" asked the agitated captain, returning in his boat. The reply from his first mate was, "We have been stove by a whale."

Chase (1797–1869) is the author of the first authentic account of the ramming and sinking of a ship by a whale. His story gives not only the details of the attack by a furious sperm whale on November 20, 1820, but covers also the three-month effort of the crew to survive in three open boats; out of twenty men, only eight lived to tell the tale. The voyage of the two boats that were picked up off South America was twice as long as that of Bligh in the *Bounty's* launch, and included even the horrors of cannibalism.

The sinking of the *Essex* by a whale is memorable not only in itself but in literary history. Herman Melville used the incident as the climax of his novel *Moby Dick* (1851), in which he mentioned the fate of Chase's ship and claimed, mistakenly, that he had talked with Chase. He did, however, meet Chase's son, from whom he received a copy of the *Narrative*.

Chase was born in Nantucket. Not long after his fourth marriage, in 1840, he retired from the sea and lived in the town of his birth until his death in 1869. His "plain and faithful narrative", in Melville's words, is objective, and in only a few details can his facts be controverted by other accounts.

An edition of Chase's work, limited to 275 copies and illustrated with twelve engravings by Robert Gibbings, was published by the Golden Cockerel Press (London, 1935). It is supplemented therein by the narrative of Thomas Chappel or Chapple printed anonymously as "An Account of the Loss of the *Essex*" (London: Religious Tract Society, No. 579, 1830), as well as a report by Captain James Pollard included in Tyerman and Bennet (see No. 40). An edition of 1963 (New York: Corinth Books) edited by Bruce R. McElderry, Jr., contains all this material, as well as illustrations, a bibliographical note (p. xx), and a facsimile and transcript of the notes in Melville's copy of Chase's book. Another illustrated reprint (New York: Harcourt, Brace and World, 1965) was edited by Iola Haverstick and Betty Shepard.

[47] C. S. STEWART. *A Visit to the South Seas, in the U.S. Ship "Vincennes", During the Years 1829 and 1830* . . . 2 vol. London: Fisher, Son & Jackson, 1832. Edited and abridged by William Ellis. New York: J. P. Haven, 1831.

Charles Samuel Stewart (1795–1870), after missionary endeavors in the Hawaiian Islands, sailed as chaplain of an American man-of-war around the globe.

Stewart, born with "great expectations" that did not materialize, was an aristocratic-looking, cheerful young man who was trained as a lawyer. A religious awakening aroused him to study theology at Princeton University, and he was sent to Hawaii by the American Board of Commissioners for Foreign Missions. He was accompanied by his wife, Harriet Bradford Tiffany, whom he had married in June, 1822, at Albany, New York. She was a descendant of William Bradford, Pilgrim governor of Plymouth, Massachusetts. They lived for two years at the port of Lahaina, Maui, where Stewart and William Richards were the first permanent preachers among twenty thousand Hawaiian residents. One result of the Stewart stay was his important volume, *Journal of a Residence in the Sandwich Islands* . . . (London: H. Fisher, Son & Jackson, 1828; also as *Private Journal of a Voyage to the Pacific*

Ocean, New York: J. P. Haven, 1828; also as *A Residence in the Sandwich Islands*, Boston: Weeks, Jordan & Co., 1839).

His wife's ill health in the tropics caused Stewart to sever his connections with the mission, but he took the opportunity to make a return visit, without his wife, to the scenes of his island labors when he became chaplain of the corvette *Vincennes* under Captain William Bolton Finch. This vessel stopped at Rio de Janeiro, passed around Cape Horn, visited Callao, Peru, and stopped at Nuku Hiva in the Marquesas, or "Washington Islands" as they were then called. Stewart's chapters on this group were strengthened by conversations with the Rev. William Pascoe Crook, who had spent nearly two years in the Marquesas and who lent Stewart a manuscript of his observations. The *Vincennes* volume was a main source for Herman Melville (see No. 51), especially for his novel *Typee*.

Stewart's familiarity with the Hawaiian Islands aided the diplomatic work of his captain. Parties from the ship climbed up to Kilauea Volcano on the island of Hawaii. The vessel then sailed to Honolulu and to Stewart's old station at Lahaina. Chapter 65 includes a report of the Hawaii visit by Captain Finch, sent to the Secretary of the Navy in November, 1829. Stewart gives some attention to Manila, Cape Town, and St. Helena, all visited on the circumnavigation from which he returned to New York in June, 1830.

Stewart's observations are contained in the form of letters to his wife, who died not many months after his return. His introduction to the American edition states: "It was not my intention . . . to present the matter in its original, familiar, and confidential form. But circumstances . . . made the review of the manuscript too unwelcome a task to admit of any material alteration either in its arrangement or style; and, with the exception of erasures, the whole remains, almost word for word, as originally penned at the common mess-table of a gun room . . . and within hearing of all the bustle and din of a man-of-war." The book thus has a quality of chatty freshness lacking in more polished narratives.

[48] EDWARD LUCETT or LUCATT. *Rovings in the Pacific, from 1837 to 1849*, by a Merchant Long Resident at Tahiti. 2 vol. London: Longman, Brown, Green & Longman, 1851.

Edward Lucett, an English merchant and shipowner, spent twelve years in the Pacific, and his comments on the many islands he visited as a trader are vivid and valuable. His anonymously published volumes describe travels to Australia, New Zealand, Rotuma, the Society and Tuamotu groups, the Gambiers, Rapa, Juan Fernández, the Hervey Islands, the Marquesas, Fanning, Christmas, Palmyra, Penrhyn, the Hawaiian Chain, and the Philippines. Lucett was an energetic traveler who frequently remarked on South Sea native and commercial life.

Lucett is known to students of Herman Melville's career in the Pacific (see No. 51) because the merchant, who had settled at Tahiti almost a year earlier than Melville's beachcombing stay, attacks the author of *Typee* and *Omoo* in his own book. "Herman Melville possesses a felicitous pen," he says, "with a humorous knack of hitting off little peculiarities of character; and if he had confined himself to these, without publishing names, or making gross aspersions upon worthy men, his works might have gone down the stream with other harmless and amusing productions; but he has passed base coin as sterling, and for so doing, deserves exposure and contempt" (II, 167–168).

Lucett apparently felt that he had just cause for his prejudice against Melville, who in October and November, 1842, resided in the Calabooza Beretanee or British jail at Papeete for refusing duty on the Australian whaleship *Lucy Ann*. On the night of November 17, Lucett was cast into the stocks in this jail by native constables on a charge of violating the curfew law. Libelously referring to a Yankee whom he identified as Melville, Lucett wrote: "Uttering a volley of oaths, the dastardly dog hereupon drew his sheath knife, and threw himself upon me, helpless as I lay. . . . Herman Melville, undoubtedly the ringleader of the mutineers, was lying in the calliboose when I was dragged there; and from the un-English way in which the ruffian who assaulted me handled his knife, I have the strongest suspicion that it was Herman Melville who threw himself upon a bound and defenseless man" (II, 287–290). Melville had departed for Mooréa, however, early in November, and presumably never met Lucett; certainly he never printed his name. The ill-mannered Yankee was probably the man Melville calls "Salem". Lucett also attacks Melville for his descriptions of Mooréa but independently supports the New Yorker's remarks concerning native constables and the rigors of the missionary regime at Papeete, which inculcated hypocrisy among the Polynesian inhabitants. Other observations by this shrewd trader should be of interest to students of South Sea life in the nineteenth century.

[49] **CHARLES WILKES.** *Narrative of the United States Exploring Expedition* . . . London: Ingram, Cooke, 1852. 2 vol. Philadelphia: C. Sherman, 1844, 5 vol.

Wilkes (1798–1877), American naval officer and explorer, born in New York, entered the Navy as a midshipman at the age of twenty and became an authority on hydrographic science. While still a lieutenant he was appointed to command the expedition authorized by Congress to make an extensive survey of the Pacific Ocean and the northwest coast of America.

The expedition was the most ambitious scientific undertaking that had hitherto been organized by any nation. It consisted of the flagship *Vincennes* and five other vessels, which set sail in 1838 and spent four years visiting most of the Pacific Island groups and surveying some 280 islands. Peaceful in intent, the expedition nevertheless encountered many adventures, and also pioneered in the mapping of the Antarctic continent. Surviving shipwrecks and attacks by natives, the Americans discovered islands in the Tuamotu, Tokelau, Ellice, and Phoenix groups. The greatest results, however, came from the work done by various noted scientists whose reports and maps were made available in a set of large illustrated volumes. Wilkes himself prepared the volumes on meteorology and hydrography and wrote the official account here listed. His *Narrative* went through six editions in eight years.

A volume on the career of Wilkes, often referred to as "the American Captain Cook", is *The Hidden Coasts* (New York: William Sloane Associates, 1953), by Daniel M. Henderson.

Another biography is Robert Silverberg's *Stormy Voyager: the Story of Charles Wilkes* (Philadelphia: Lippincott, 1968).

[50] FRANCIS ALLYN OLMSTED. *Incidents of a Whaling Voyage. . . .* London: John Neale, 1844. New York: D. Appleton, 1841.

Olmsted's book was the most popular description of the whaling industry previous to the publication of Herman Melville's *Moby Dick* (see No. 51). Olmsted's account of his voyage is certainly to be listed among the Pacific classics.

Francis Allyn Olmsted (1819–1844) was the son of a versatile professor at the University of North Carolina, who was later appointed to teach at Yale. Just graduated from that college, young Olmsted took to the sea in search of improved health in a milder climate. He boarded the *North America* at New London, Connecticut, in October, 1839. The ship hunted whales in the Atlantic and then rounded Cape Horn, heading for the Hawaiian Islands. Olmsted's account of that region resulted in "one of the wittiest pictures of Hawaii created prior to the visit of Mark Twain". The *North America* next visited Tahiti, the South Pacific, and again Cape Horn, and returned home after almost a year and a half. The ship suffered various disasters and adventures and made a fair catch of whales.

Olmsted, greatly improved in health, returned in February, 1841, and prepared a manuscript based on his journal. It was illustrated with etchings which were later hailed as the most vivid representations of whaling ever drawn. The publisher rushed the book to the press the same year. Olmsted entered Yale as a graduate medical student in the autumn, but again his studies proved too exhausting, and again he took a cruise, this time to the Caribbean. The climate there did not have the healing properties of that of the Pacific, and Olmsted, with a medical degree conferred upon him *in absentia*, returned to Connecticut early in the summer of 1844 and died a few weeks later, only five days after his twenty-fifth birthday.

A recent reprint of Olmsted's entertaining work, with a preface by W. Storrs Lee, was published with the co-operation of Friends of the Library, Maui, Hawaii (Rutland, Vermont, and Tokyo: Charles E. Tuttle, 1969).

[51] HERMAN MELVILLE. *Narrative of a Four Months' Residence Among the Natives in a Valley of the Marquesas Islands.* London: John Murray, 1846. *Typee: a Peep at Polynesian Life.* New York: Wiley & Putnam, 1846.

Melville (1819–1891), whom his English biographer, John Freeman, called "the most powerful of all the great American writers", set his six most important works in the Pacific region. *Typee* (issued first in London with a long title) is the first of Melville's books and, with the exception of *Moby Dick,* is the most widely read.

Melville entered the Pacific around Cape Horn in mid-April, 1841, and spent more than three years there as whaleman, mutineer, beachcomber, and foremast hand in the United States Navy. He deserted from the whale ship *Acushnet* of New Bedford with a fellow crewman, Richard Tobias Greene, at Nuku Hiva in the Marquesas group on July 9, and climbed over hills through rain forest to the forbidding valley of Taipi or "Typee". Despite their reputation as ferocious cannibals, the Polynesian tribesmen took them in and Melville, who suffered a leg infection, was cared for tenderly. Toby went for help and was never able to return to the valley. Melville enjoyed the primitive life of the people, but after less than a month he escaped to an Australian whale ship.

Subsequent events are told in *Omoo: a Narrative of Adventures in the South Seas* (London: John Murray, 1847; New York: Harper, 1847), which deals with the mutiny of the *Julia* and Melville's wanderings on Tahiti and Mooréa (which he calls by the older name of "Imeeo" or Eimeo). His third book, *Mardi: and a Voyage Thither,* 3 vol. (London: Richard Bentley, 1849; New York: 2 vol., Harper, 1849) begins as a sea story but turns into an allegory during which the narrator, Taji, and his friends tour an imaginary Pacific archipelago. Each island provides material for satire on nations or customs. Melville's fifth book, *White-Jacket: or The World in a Man-Of-War* (London: Richard Bentley, 1850; New York, Harper, 1850), is an account of his service as an

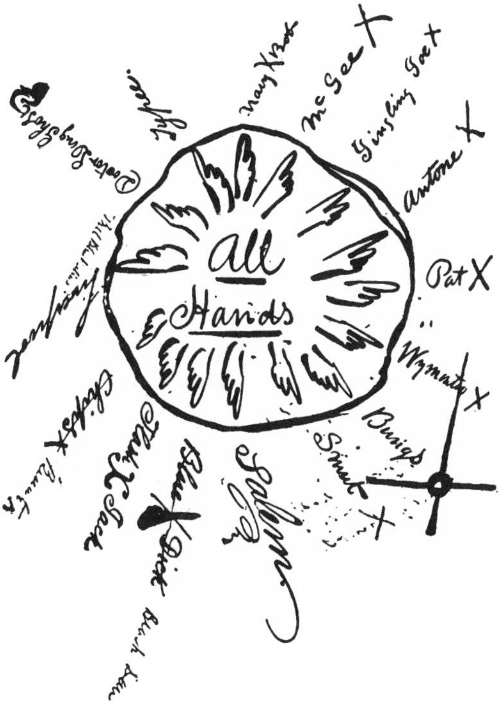

Melville, who signed himself "Typee," was among the "ringleaders" who signed the mutinous round robin aboard the *Lucy Ann* at Tahiti, as told in chapter 20 of *Omoo*.

enlisted man aboard the U.S.S. *United States*, on which he returned around the Horn and was discharged in Boston in October, 1844. The later chapters of *The Whale*, 3 vol. (London: Richard Bentley, 1851; *Moby-Dick; or, The Whale*, New York: Harper, 1851) are enacted in the Pacific. A series of ten sketches called "The Encantadas, or Enchanted Isles", dealing with the equatorial Galápagos Islands of the Pacific, appeared in *Putnam's Magazine* in 1854 and was collected in *The Piazza-Tales* (London: Sampson Low, 1856; New York: Dix & Edwards, 1856). Melville made another visit to the Pacific in 1860, sailing around Cape Horn on the clipper *Meteor*, commanded by his brother Thomas; Herman disembarked at San Francisco and soon returned to New York via the Isthmus of Panama. A lecture on "The South Seas" was Melville's mainstay on the platform for several years. He also wrote several poems and sections of his long poem *Clarel* (1876) about South Sea experiences.

Numerous reprints of Melville's works, including *Typee*, have appeared. Most of them contain gross errors. The most reliable text of *Typee* is that edited by Harrison Hayford *et al.* (Evanston and Chicago: Northwestern University Press and The Newberry Library, 1968), first in a proposed critical edition of fifteen volumes. *Omoo* also appeared in this series during the same year; *Mardi* appeared in 1970. The standard edition in sixteen volumes (London: Constable, 1922–1924) was reprinted in New York by Russell & Russell in 1963.

Melville was the first author of genius to use the South Seas as material, and most of those who followed saw the region through his eyes and adopted his patterns. Since the revival of Melville during the 1920s, a library of books and articles has explored almost every incident of his life and cranny of his mind. No recent bibliography of Melvilleana is available; the most complete checklist to 1956 is found in the hardbound edition of *The Fine Hammered Steel of Herman Melville* by Milton R. Stern (Urbana, Ill.: University of Illinois Press, 1957), 252–291. Among the list, the most valuable ones on the Pacific are Charles R. Anderson, *Melville in the South Seas* (New York: Columbia University Press, 1939; softbound, New York: Dover Publications, 1966) and James Baird, *Ishmael* (Baltimore, Md.: The Johns Hopkins Press, 1956). An anthology, *Melville's South Seas* (New York: Hawthorn Books, 1970), with lengthy introductory essays, is edited by A. Grove Day.

[52] A. GROVE DAY and CARL STROVEN (eds.). *Best South Sea Stories.* London: Souvenir Press, 1964. New York: Appleton-Century, 1964.

Fifteen outstanding short stories ranging in time from Herman Melville to Eugene Burdick are presented with introductions.

Other authors include W. Somerset Maugham, John Russell, James Norman Hall, Jack London, James A. Michener, Robert Dean Frisbie, R. L. Stevenson, Lloyd Osbourne, Charles Warren Stoddard, Sir Arthur Grimble, Frank Bullen, and Louis Becke.

Messrs. Day and Stroven, classmates at Stanford University, California, and fellow professors in the Department of English at the University of Hawaii, produced five anthologies of Pacific literature. Others dealing with the broad region are *The Spell of the Pacific* (New York: Macmillan, 1949) and *True Tales of the South Seas* (London: Souvenir Press, 1967; New York: Appleton-Century, 1966). Dr. Day also wrote several books of Pacific history, including *Adventurers of the Pacific* (New York: Meredith Press, 1969).

Aside from the pioneer anthology of E. C. Parnwell, *Stories of the South Seas* (London: Oxford University Press, World's Classics No. 332, 1928), stories have been collected by Christina Stead (*Great Stories of the South Sea Islands*, London: F. Muller, 1955) and Philip Snow (*Best Stories of the South Seas*, London: Faber & Faber, 1967).

[53] "WILLIAM DIAPEA". *Cannibal Jack: the True Autobiography of a White Man in the South Seas*. London: Faber & Gwyer, 1928. New York: G. P. Putnam, 1928.

William James Diaper (1820–1891), alias Diapea, alias John Jackson, alias Cannibal Jack, alias Silver Eyes, spent most of his lengthy life as a beachcomber and pioneer on a moving South Sea frontier. His ability as a linguist and his adaptable understanding of non-white people made him a notable early figure in many island regions.

Diaper was born at Ardleigh, Essex, on November 11, 1820. He probably attended the grammar school at Dedham; he was a born writer and one of the few literate beachcombers. He left England early, "like thousands of others before me, . . . trying to run away from myself, or chasing shadows". He adopted the unremarkable name of "John Jackson", and even used on his manuscript the slight variant of "Diapea" for his patronymic.

He claimed to have written his life story "in nineteen common copybooks", most of them lost. His early career is told in Appendix A, "Jackson's Narrative", in J. H. Erskine's *Journal of a Cruise Among the Islands of the Western Pacific . . . in Her Majesty's Ship "Havannah"* (London: John Murray, 1853; Dawson, 1967). While on a whaling voyage in 1840 he was kidnapped, according to this narrative, by the Samoans of Manua, who wanted him as their resident white man. Several months later he left for Fiji, and spent seven years in that dangerous group. He was adopted by a chief and accompanied him through parts of Vanua Levu never before visited by a European; his remarks are valuable early sources on Fiji.

The manuscript of *Cannibal Jack*, consisting of Books 9, 16, and 17, was given by Diaper to the Rev. James Hadfield on Maré, Loyalty Islands, in 1889, when the writer was almost seventy. *Cannibal Jack* continues the autobiography from 1843 to the end of 1847, including Diaper's residence with his four wives at Natewa, Fiji, and his stays at Futuna, the Lau group, and Tonga. He then voyaged to Manila to sell tortoiseshell. The latter section deals with his three attempts to sail from Fiji to Tonga by canoe and events in Ha'apai and Vava'u.

After the episodes narrated in the book, Diaper lived in New Caledonia and the New Hebrides, and returned to Samoa and Fiji. He settled on Maré in the Loyalties, where he died in 1891. Diaper is one of the outstanding figures included in Chapter IV, "Beachcombers and Castaways", in *Of Islands and Men* by H. E. Maude (London and Melbourne: Oxford University Press, 1968). In an excellent study, "William Diaper: A Biographical Sketch", *Journal of Pacific History*, I, 1966, 79–90, by Christopher Legge, which corrects some of Diaper's printed dates and several "facts", the author concludes: "Long outdating the heyday of the true beachcomber, Diaper was compelled, as were others of his class, to change his occupations to accord with economic developments in the area in which he lived; and we find the man who had cast bullets for native warfare, copied sermons for missionaries, boiled blubber for whalers, bred pigs, sawn sandalwood, and interpreted for naval captains, becoming a sugar plantation overseer." Diaper's two vivid narratives are quite authentic and stirring accounts of adventure during the beachcombing era.

[54] CHARLES ROBERT DARWIN. *Journal of Researches into the Geology and Natural History of the Various Countries Visited During the Voyage of H.M.S. "Beagle" Round the World.* 2 vol. London: Henry Colburn, 1839. New York: Harper, 1846.

Darwin (1809–1882), the greatest English naturalist, studying for the ministry at Cambridge University, became aroused to observe the physical world. The critical point in his life was his decision to sail as naturalist on H.M.S. *Beagle* on a surveying expedition which lasted from December, 1831, to October, 1836. This circumnavigation prepared him for his life work of enunciating revolutionary biological theories, based frequently on his experiences in the Pacific. As Darwin wrote in his autobiography: "The voyage of the *Beagle* has been by far the most important event in my life, and has determined my whole career. . . . Everything about which I thought or read was made to bear directly on what I had seen or was likely to see; and this habit of mind was continued during the five years of the voyage. I feel sure that it was this training which has enabled me to do whatever I have done in science."

In the Pacific the ship's company explored the Galápagos Islands, New Zealand, Australia, and Tasmania. Darwin's journal reports observations which led to his theory of natural selection, and also forms the basis for his theory of the formation of coral islands, which is still the most widely accepted one. It is interesting that Alfred Russel Wallace, who enunciated the idea of the origin of species almost simultaneously with Darwin, also based many of his demonstrations on Pacific fauna and flora. The journal of the *Beagle* voyage is still highly readable as an account of the adventures of a brilliant young scientist. Reprints are readily available. An abridgment by Millicent E. Selsam, illustrated by Anthony Ravielli, is entitled *The Voyage of the "Beagle"* (London: Hamish Hamilton, 1962; New York: Harper & Row, 1959).

[55] EDWARD T. PERKINS. *Na Motu; or, Reef-Rovings in the South Seas. . . .* New York: Pudney & Russell, 1854.

Edward T. Perkins sailed to the Pacific aboard the whale ship *Planet* in 1848. He left her at Honolulu and spent twenty months in the Hawaiian group, before sailing to the Society Islands. Since *na motu* signifies "the islands" in both the Hawaiian and Tahitian languages, Perkins considered these words a suitable title for this account of his wanderings.

In the opening chapters on whaling, the author avoided "the hackneyed routine of ship-duty" in favor of "a combination of nautical incidents, grave and humorous". Much of the Hawaiian material offers valuable sidelights on the period. In the Society group, Perkins sojourned for some time on Raiatéa and Bora Bora before settling at Tahiti. He remarks on the town of Papeete, the Broom Road, Point Venus, the native girls and family life, a trip to a mountain lake, and the quirks of the French protectorate. While returning by schooner to Raiatéa, Perkins went ashore at Mooréa and conversed with a carpenter who claimed to remember Herman Melville and "Long Ghost" (see No. 51). Perkins concludes with a discussion of missionary efforts in the Pacific, to counter "the influence of evil reports that have gone abroad".

In his appendixes Perkins forsakes his chatty style and gives useful factual information on Polynesia, the Hawaiian Islands, the French in the Pacific, and American whaling interests in that ocean. His national bias is revealed in a preface, in which he states: "At no period of our national existence have American interests been so prominently manifest in the great Western Ocean. Laws, literature, and commerce are results of an enterprise that has established states and successfully combated a national antipathy. . . . A candid observer who surveys the broad track of American enterprise in this ocean will seek in vain for beacons of selfish cupidity or ambition. . . . To kingdoms and tribes we have bequeathed indelible impressions of our national worth and disinterested philanthropy."

Title page of *Na Motu* drawn by the author, E. T. Perkins.

[56] THOMAS HENRY HUXLEY. *Diary of the Voyage of H.M.S. "Rattlesnake"*. London: Chatto & Windus, 1935. New York: Doubleday, Doran, 1936.

Not only Darwin but "Darwin's bulldog", Thomas Henry Huxley (1825–1895), obtained early experience in biological research on scientific expeditions to the South Seas. Huxley, one of the greatest English scientists, as a young man spent almost five years (1846–1850) as assistant surgeon on the exploring vessel *Rattlesnake* in the South Pacific (see No. 40). His fascination with the flora and fauna of this region made him decide to become a biologist rather than a medical practitioner. In the Pacific he found not only a future career but a wife, Henrietta Heathorne of Sydney, Australia. Huxley Island in the Louisiade Archipelago was given his name.

The young naturalist's journal, edited by his grandson Julian Huxley, reveals the literary skill that was to make him the most readable biologist of his generation. Huxley's naval post as medical officer allowed him time to reap a collection of specimens in the waters of Australia and Melanesia, where the *Rattlesnake* under Captain Owen Stanley was making surveys. The journal also recounts incidents such as the rescue of Mrs. Thompson, who had survived drowning on Possession Island and lived for five years among the cannibals of the islands near the tip of Cape York.

[57] E. H. LAMONT. *Wild Life Among the Pacific Islanders.* London: Hurst and Blackett, 1867.

Literature by traders in the Pacific is scarce, but one book is outstanding. Lamont was a businessman from San Francisco whose cargo was easily sold in Tahiti. On his return voyage he was wrecked in 1853 on isolated Tongareva or Penrhyn Island, northwest of the Society Group. He spent some months among the people of the atoll (two of whom he married), took part in the skirmishes between the occupants of the various islets, and built a sailing vessel on which he and the other survivors could take outings. As he had no wares to sell, before being rescued he occupied his time in recording the lives of these Polynesian people.

Warriors dancing on the *marae*, or sacred ground, at Penrhyn Island.

Sir Peter Buck in his *Introduction to Polynesian Anthropology* (Honolulu: Bernice P. Bishop Museum, Bulletin 187, 1945) calls Lamont's book "the best first-hand account of an atoll community".

A connection is found between Lamont's book and Melville's *Omoo* (see No. 51), whose hero is "Doctor Long Ghost" or John Troy. After joining the California gold rush, Troy shipped out with Lamont on the *Chatham* as "Dr. R——". After the wreck on Penrhyn Island, the "doctor" aided in the theft of the only boat, making off in the direction of Chile, and was later reported a resident in a South American coastal city.

[58] HOUSTON BRANCH and FRANK WATERS.

Diamond Head. New York: Farrar, Straus, 1948.

Whaleships in the Pacific suffered heavy mortality during the Civil War. The celebrated Confederate raider *Shenandoah* was viciously active in 1865. Almost the entire New England whaling fleet was hunting among the ice floes of the Bering Sea grounds when the *Shenandoah* attacked. Captain James I. Waddell was notified that General Robert E. Lee had surrendered and that any further destruction of unarmed ships would be piracy. Many vessels, laden with oil and bone at the end of the season, were easy prey. On one day, eleven of them were captured and most were burned, while the helpless crews watched with rage. Waddell was notified three times that the war was over, but in all he destroyed twenty-five ships of the Arctic fleet, and the whaling industry of the past century never completely recovered from this blow.

A romantic novel about the voyage of the *Shenandoah* has been woven by two American fiction writers. As a last desperate effort to cut off the Union supply of whale oil, two young Confederate naval officers are sent on a mission to find the rendezvous of the whaling fleet. Lieutenant John Kirby gets himself shanghaied aboard a whaler as a foremast hand. Lieutenant Cameron Richards flees to England and there joins the *Shenandoah* on her vengeful cruise. Scenes range from Richmond, New Bedford, England, Australia, and Hawaii to the Arctic Circle. History is modified to permit the *Shenandoah* to refit at Hawaii instead of Melbourne, Australia, perhaps to enable Richards to carry on a love affair with Abigail, daughter of the Yankee sea captain Jireh Macy. Those who enjoy semi-historical fiction will be pleased with *Diamond Head* and its story of the last battle of the Civil War.

A later novel about the *Shenandoah*, based on extensive documentation, is James D. Horan's *Seek Out and Destroy* (New York: Crown, 1959), which again stresses the attempt by the Confederate Navy to turn the tide of defeat. A non-fiction account by one of the ship's officers is *The Shenandoah: or The Last Confederate Cruiser* (New York: G. W. Carleton, 1867) by Cornelius E. Hunt.

[59] R. W. ROBSON. *Queen Emma.* Sydney: Pacific Publications, 1965.

"Queen" Emma Coe Kolbe, whose father was an American trader and whose mother was a Samoan lady of the Malietoa line, was notorious in the black islands of Melanesia as a pioneer builder of a million-dollar coconut kingdom. This true story of the vivacious Emma touches many other episodes of South Sea life in the empire-building days.

Growing up as a lovely, high-spirited Samoan princess, educated in Sydney and San Francisco, Emma freely mingled love and politics. She pulled wires in Samoa during the reign there of her lover Colonel Albert Barnes Steinberger, for whose sake she granted to the United States the lands at Pago Pago on which the American naval base stands today. Although married to a British trading captain, Emma strangely joined forces with burly, red-bearded Tom Farrell and fled to the cannibal-infested Duke of York Islands. The pair built on the New Britain coast the most famous mansion in the South Seas and sheltered the survivors of the tragic Marquis de Rays colonization fraud (see No. 74). Emma got possession of rich plantation lands before Germany annexed the region, and built a trading principality for her only son. After Farrell departed the scene, and her brother and her giant Dalmatian lover Tino Stalio were murdered by natives of the Fead group, Emma made her peace with the Germans and even married a German officer; both died mysteriously at Monte Carlo on the eve of World War I. The factual accounts of Emma's escapades are more incredible than the gossip that trailed behind her during her restless career. Descendants of the Coe clan are still dwelling in the South Pacific today.

Robert William Robson was born in 1885 at Wyndham, New Zealand, eldest of a family of fourteen children of bush settlers. Since no school was available, Robson got his education from his mother, from a Presbyterian lay minister, and—when he was working in a bakery in his teens—in night classes at an Invercargill high school. Young Robson began working on a newspaper when he was twenty, and thereafter journalism was his career—in New Zealand, Australia, England, and the South Pacific. He was founder of the *Pacific Islands Monthly* in 1930. His company later acquired Pacific Publications Pty. Ltd. and the Fiji Times and Herald Ltd. During half a century of travel in the Pacific, Mr. Robson collected many strange tales; none is more fascinating than that of "Queen" Emma, which is based on years of fact-seeking around the world.

[60] [EARL OF PEMBROKE and DR. HENRY KINGSLEY.] *South Sea Bubbles.* By the Earl and the Doctor. London: R. Bentley, 1872. New York: D. Appleton, 1872.

In the days before dozens of people sailed in yachts through the South Seas and published their logs and snapshots, a volume by a British peer and a distinguished medical man was highly popular.

George Robert Charles Herbert (1850–1895), thirteenth Earl of Pembroke, and Dr. George Henry Kingsley (1827–1892), brother of novelists Charles and Henry Kingsley, sailed together on the yacht *Albatross* in 1870. Their collaboration covers visits at Tahiti, Mooréa, Huahine, Raiatea, Bora Bora, Tubuai, Rarotonga, and Samoa. In Apia the twenty-year-old Earl was served kava prepared by the beauteous young "princess", Emma Coe (see No. 59). He managed to arrange an evening fantasia during which his princess and five other girls were "frisking and gambadoing in the most fearful manner . . . making the very coco-trees above our heads bristle with horror!". Although regretting that he should have stayed in Samoa, the Earl ordered the *Albatross* to sail for the Fiji group. The yacht was wrecked on October 21, 1870, on a reef at Nukumbasanga, in the northwestern part of the Ringgold Isles. It broke up in a few days, but the Earl's manuscripts and other valuables were salvaged. After camping ashore, all hands took to three overladen boats, which at the end of the month saw the coast of Taveuni and were rescued by a schooner in Somosomo Strait. "If I were to rewrite this article I could make quite a romantic story of it, without much alteration or exaggeration," the Earl remarks; "but I vowed a vow to use no rouge or pencils, and . . . I have kept my oath."

The tone of *South Sea Bubbles* is frothy and the narrative is laden with literary allusions, becoming to a scion of the famed Herbert family of Wilton House in Wiltshire. Reprobation of missionaries in the final chapter gave offense to some readers, who objected to such statements as: "The crude truth is that nine-tenths of foreign missions are not got up for the benefit of the heathen abroad, but for the good of the sect at home."

[61] CHARLES WARREN STODDARD. *Summer Cruising in the South Seas.* London: Chatto & Windus, 1874. *South-Sea Idylls.* Boston: James R. Osgood, 1873.

One of the circle of young San Franciscan writers that included Bret Harte, Mark Twain, and Ambrose Bierce was Charles Warren Stoddard (1843–1909). At first he wrote poetry only, but encouraged by Bret Harte he turned to writing prose sketches, some of them deriving from his several trips to the South Seas. In 1870 he sailed for the Society Islands on a French man-of-war.

The best of his various volumes, *South-Sea Idylls*, was taken as a contribution to the local-color movement popular in the United States in the latter part of the last century. It contained "A Prodigal in Tahiti", about which William Dean Howells, who accepted the story for the *Atlantic Monthly*, wrote to the author many years later, "I think, now, that there are few such delicious bits of literature in the language."

After a childhood in his birthplace, Rochester, New York, Stoddard lived in San Francisco, and was probably the one person who inspired Robert Louis Stevenson to spend his later years in the Pacific region. Of him Stevenson observed: "There are but two writers who have touched the South Seas with genius, both Americans: Melville and Charles Warren Stoddard."

Stoddard's writings are usually dreamy sketches of a land where it is "always afternoon". Of them Howells wrote that they are "graceful shapes, careless, beautiful, with a kind of undying youth in them".

[62] LAWRENCE KLINGMAN and GERALD GREEN. *His Majesty O'Keefe.* London: Hale, 1952. New York: Scribner, 1950.

The legendary white ruler of the island of Yap in the Caroline group, David Dean O'Keefe, is brought to life in this stirring historical novel based on research in obscure places.

O'Keefe, a gigantic, carrot-haired Irishman, is about forty years old when, in the early 1870s, he flees his family in Savannah, Georgia, because he thinks he has killed a drunken crewman on his steamer. Cast up on Yap and tutored by the tribal magician Fatumak, O'Keefe attains power on this overlooked island, mainly by controlling the traffic in *fei*, stone wheels used as symbols of Yapese wealth. He obtains a Chinese junk and names it *Katherine*, after his deserted wife. He is revered by the native people, who are rewarded by stone wheels quarried on Palau and other islands and transported to Yap. They raise copra to be sold in Hong Kong. O'Keefe, by trading in the region, defeating "Bully" Hayes when Yap is invaded by the piratical crew of the blackbirder *Leonora*, and evading the colonizers of Spain, Germany, and Britain, builds up a fleet and a South Sea "empire". He marries a half-native girl, Dalabo, and rears a new family; the daughters are still remembered in Micronesia for their beauty. When the Germans at last take over at the end of his reign, O'Keefe flees with two of his sons. Presumed lost in the great typhoon of 1901, "King" O'Keefe becomes a demigod. "It is said that, in a remote corner of the Pacific known only to himself, he discovered another island, pristine and flourishing, where he started all over again and where he founded a dynasty which rules to this day."

The authors, in this successful collaboration, used a number of actual characters, white and brown, in their novel, which is based on research reported in their preface. As Fletcher Pratt observes: "The authors have succeeded in the almost incredible feat of welding fiction and fact together so closely that it is impossible to detect the joint in any given instance, and at the same time they have produced a book that is both fascinating narrative and a footnote to history." Of the style of the book, James A. Michener remarks that it "exactly suits the story. When historical background is needed, the authors have provided it in solid passages that could have been lifted right out of the Pacific Pilot. When anthropological data are necessary, they are given." The region covered is today part of the United States Trust Territory of the Pacific Islands. *His Majesty O'Keefe* was made into a popular color film of the same name.

[63] "PIERRE LOTI." *The Marriage of Loti.* Translated by Clara Bell. London: T. Werner Laurie, 1925; New York: F. A. Stokes, 1925.

Louis Marie Julien Viaud, better known by his pen name of "Pierre Loti" (1850–1923), was born at Rochefort, France. After preliminary education he entered the French Navy in 1870 as a midshipman. He made a brilliant reputation as a writer of exotic novels based on experiences and impressions gained from his visits to many strange ports around the world. Settings in his best known books are Iceland, Japan, Morocco, Angkor, and Tahiti. None had greater influence in creating the *mirage* of an exotic South Seas than *Rarahu* (1880); the title was changed in 1882 to *Tahiti: Le Mariage de Loti.*

This semi-autobiographical novel describes a young midshipman's sojourn in Tahiti in 1872 and his love affair with Rarahu, a Polynesian girl attached to the court of Pomaré, the old Tahitian queen. Loti caught in this book the sensuous luxuriance of tropical nature and the spirit of a primitive people when their way of life, under the impact of Western civilization, was inevitably chang-

An etching by Pierre Loti of the dancing girls of dreamy Tahiti.

ing. No book published since has had more influence in determing the tone and viewpoint of South Sea fiction and travel literature.

[64] FRANK T. BULLEN. *The Cruise of the "Cachalot".* London: Smith, Elder, 1898; New York: A. L. Burt, 1898.

Frank Thomas Bullen (1857–1915), an orphan who spent his boyhood dodging about London as a ragged street Arab "with wits sharpened by the constant fight for food", took to the sea when he was thirteen and sailed to many parts of the world. Stranded and penniless in New Bedford, Massachusetts, in 1875, he signed articles on an American whaling ship bound for the Pacific. Years later, after he had left the sea to become a clerk in London, he told the story of this voyage in his first book, which ranks next to Melville's *Moby Dick* among the classic novels on whaling. Those who can be fascinated by the adventures that befall the "blubber hunter" in the Pacific in the later years of the sailing ships will be charmed by Bullen's candor and his vivid recollections of rough days in search of the elusive sea monsters. Bullen's other books—fiction and reminiscences—have been largely forgotten, but *The Cruise of the "Cachalot"* is a classic.

[65] CONSTANCE F. GORDON-CUMMING. *A Lady's Cruise in a French Man-of-War.* 2 vol. London: Blackwood, 1882.

In a series of chatty letters, a much-traveled English lady wrote of her experiences among several of the Pacific groups. The feminine view of the South Seas has rarely been given with greater verve.

When Sir Arthur Hamilton Gordon was appointed first governor of Fiji in 1875, Miss Constance Frederica Gordon-Cumming, of a prominent Scottish family, accompanied Lady Gordon to that Crown Colony. Her two-year stay is reported in her book, *At Home in Fiji*, 2 vol. (London: Blackwood, 1881; New York: A. C. Armstrong, 1882). She was then invited by Monseigneur Elloi, the Catholic bishop of Samoa, to go with him on a large French war vessel, *Seignelay*, commanded by Captain Aube, to examine the diocese and show the flag. Her adventures are told in *A Lady's Cruise in a French Man-of-War*, which was reprinted in several editions.

The ship departed from Fiji on September 5, 1877. The lady was made comfortable in one of the officer's cabins, and was welcomed in every part of the trim vessel. She thought the most novel sight of all was "serving out rations, and seeing wine pumped up from huge vats, to fill the small barrels, each of which represents eight men's daily allowance".

The *Seignelay* visited Tonga, where Miss Gordon-Cumming sketched the curious trilithon and from a boat saw the famed lover's cave described by Will Mariner (see No. 35). The itinerary also included the Wallis Islands, the Samoan group (which the lady toured and where she met the two daughters of the notorious "Bully" Hayes), and Tahiti.

The second volume is devoted to Tahiti, where Miss Gordon-Cumming enjoyed a prolonged stay with a "fine family of real old Tahitian chiefs". An extensive description of the Society group at this period is supplemented by drawings by the lady herself. The *Seignelay* sailed for Valparaiso on February 9, 1878, breaking up a companionship of five months with the hospitable French seamen. Soon thereafter came the news of the terrible hurricane and tidal wave that struck the Tuamotu group. Miss Gordon-Cumming sailed on a brigantine laden with a cargo of Tahitian oranges, and at Eastertide reached San Francisco, intending to go from there by steamer to the Hawaiian group.

[66] WILLIAM E. GILES. *A Cruize in a Queensland Labour Vessel to the South Seas.* Edited by Deryck Scarr. Pacific History Series: No. 1. Canberra: Australian National University Press, 1968; Honolulu: University of Hawaii Press, 1968; London: C. Hurst, 1968.

More than sixty thousand Melanesians, mostly from the New Hebrides and the Solomons, were recruited between 1869 and 1906 to work on the Queensland plantations of Australia. This previously unpublished manuscript by a passenger on the brigantine *Bobtail Nag* in 1877 is a highly informative account of the "blackbirding" trade, which ended when the Federation decided that imported laborers were a threat to the living standards of white Australians.

During a cruise of 118 days, the crew of the *Bobtail Nag* lured aboard 110 "kanakas", who were attracted by promises of liquor, tobacco, muskets, and foreign travel. Giles, who later operated a plantation with South Seas labor, was not as much against recruiting as the official government agent aboard, who was supposed to enforce regulations and who mentioned "the odium which must ever be attached to those who are intimately connected with the trade". Despite the presence of such an agent, abuses and accidents occurred on the beaches and aboard ship. The banning in 1882 of gifts to the natives slowed down the trade considerably. Giles, as Dr. Scarr points out, undoubtedly overstresses the lasting impact of blackbirding on Melanesian history. As G. S. Parson concludes in a review, "In these years men died just as quickly at home as they did abroad. The great majority of those who went were in any case unmarried and had no prospects of marriage. Their absence did not therefore affect the birth rate or greatly alter the political balance. . . . The great migration was thus little more than a hiatus in the life of Melanesia, an episode rather than a turning point"—*Journal of Pacific History*, IV, 1969, 232–33.

[67] ANDREW FARRELL, compiler. *John Cameron's Odyssey*. London and New York: Macmillan, 1928.

Captain John Cameron (1850–1925), born in Scotland, went to sea at the age of seventeen and for thirty years sailed the Atlantic, Indian, and Pacific Oceans. His yarn, transcribed by Andrew Farrell from his own manuscript, is a lively true story of adventure in the windjammer days.

Cameron, naturalized as an American citizen in San Francisco in 1878, sailed to Honolulu on the *City of Sydney*. After knocking about he got a berth as able seaman on the brig *Pomare*, Captain Tripp, on a "blackbirding" or labor-recruiting voyage for the Kingdom of Hawaii. After various mishaps, including grounding on the reef of Nukunau in the Gilberts, the ship returned to Honolulu in February, 1881, with eighty-seven native laborers from the New Hebrides—the first Melanesians to be brought to work on the plantations of Hawaii. Cameron then became master of a cattle vessel to Tahiti, and later served as an officer in inter-island steamships in the Hawaiian group, thus making the acquaintance of King Kalakaua. As master of the *Planter* he lost his ship on Niihau. He installed machinery at the Mormon-owned sugar mill at Laie on windward Oahu, but again the sea called.

Cameron's greatest adventure came when he signed on as first mate of the British bark *Wandering Minstrel* under Captain Frederick Dunbar Walker for a shark-fishing cruise among the northwestern islands of the Hawaiian chain. The fated vessel sailed from Honolulu on December 10, 1887. At Midway Island the crew anchored and set up equipment for treating captured sharks. Ashore, Cameron rescued and listened to the story of the Crusoe of Midway, Adolph Jorgensen, a Danish carpenter who had been left behind by the crew of the wrecked schooner *General Siegel* on an earlier sharking expedition. The *Minstrel*, manned by a mutinous crew, ended her wandering during a hurricane at a poor anchorage, and Cameron joined the castaways of Midway Island.

Although Jorgensen had been accused of murder by his crew mates, Cameron chose him as a partner to head for help in an open boat, along with Moses, a Chinese boy who was "young, fat, and probably tender". After eight months on barren Midway, the trio departed on Friday, October 13, 1888—an unlucky date. However, by skillful navigation, Cameron brought their frail craft to Mili Atoll in the southern Marshall group on November 25, after forty-three days on the waters of the Pacific. Four months later, the survivors on Midway were picked up by the schooner *Norma*. The *Wandering Minstrel* mystery inspired the novel *The Wrecker* by Robert Louis Stevenson and Lloyd Osbourne (see No. 70). Cameron met the Stevensons in the steamer *Janet Nicol* on Tarawa in the Gilberts and told his side of the story.

Many other escapades are narrated by Cameron, including his narrow escape from execution by the Spanish officials at Ponape on a charge of selling arms to the natives of the Carolines. At

"Apamama" (Abemama) in the Gilberts, Cameron met "King Tem Binoka" and had a brush with the piratical brothers De Greves, alias Rorique. After serving as a South Sea trader, Cameron became owner of the schooner *Ebon* and took her on a two-year shark-fishing voyage of more than nine thousand miles from Kusaie to Japan, touching once more at his old Crusoe island of Midway as well as other scattered islands.

Cameron sold the *Ebon* in Japan around 1895 and settled down in that country for the remainder of his life. In 1897 he sailed as master of a yacht that was delivered to some Russians at Vladivostok despite a typhoon. That exploit ended his thirty years at sea. He took a shore job at Kobe with the Standard Oil Company of New York in 1899 and continued with that corporation for more than a quarter of a century, retiring a month or so before his death. He made three trips away from Japan as a passenger: to Scotland in 1911 across Siberia by rail; to New York via the Suez Canal in 1920; and to Honolulu in 1923.

The old seaman spent three weeks in December, 1923, in Honolulu, passing some time with his "transcriber", Andrew Farrell, a newspaper man who had agreed to boil down a 988-page manuscript and put it in publishable book form. "In my mind's eye," remembered Farrell, "I can still see the old fellow, boyish-hearted at seventy-four, stocky, deep-chested, broad, powerful, with a white thatch and white mustache and beard, a sparkle in his gray eye." Captain Cameron died before he had read more than a few pages of his odyssey as retold, but Farrell checked the typescript with Mrs. Cameron. He also had at hand a number of letters written by the captain to a friend in Honolulu, and added to the book a number of highly valuable notes that confirm most of Cameron's statements. The Scotsman, like a good trader, although sometimes vague about exact dates, balanced his emotional books cannily. Apparently he always rewarded a good turn but never let an injury go unrequited. The result of the Cameron-Farrell collaboration is an anecdotal yarn for many dogwatches, in a style as salty as lobscouse.

[68] LOUIS BECKE. *By Reef and Palm.* London: T. Fisher Unwin, Autonym Library, 1894. Philadelphia: J. B. Lippincott, 1900.

George Lewis Becke (1855–1913), under the pseudonym of "Louis Becke", is generally acclaimed as the best writer of South Sea stories to have lived for many years in the region he evoked in fact and fiction.

After spending two decades as a trader, beachcomber, blackbirder, and wanderer "from Rapa to Palau", Becke at the age of thirty-eight began to write stories for the famed Sydney *Bulletin*, and in 1896 went to London to embark on a literary career. Before his death in his native Australia, to which he returned in 1908, he published thirty-five books about the Pacific, six of them in collaboration with Walter James Jeffery.

Becke is best remembered for the tales drawn from his years of residence on various islands, of which *By Reef and Palm* (with an undependable introduction by the Earl of Pembroke—see No. 60) is only the first of a dozen almost equally alluring. This brief book is often bound along with Becke's second collection, *The Ebbing of the Tide: South Sea Stories* (London: Unwin, 1895; Philadelphia: Lippincott, 1900). Becke was seldom able to sustain the pace in a novel, although the structure of *The Mutineer: A Romance of Pitcairn Island* (London: Unwin, 1898), probably the contribution of his collaborator Jeffery, is sound, and the interest focuses on the character of Fletcher Christian throughout. Becke's final novel, *The Adventures of Louis Blake* (London: T. Werner Laurie, 1909; Philadelphia: Lippincott, 1926) is his best; it is semi-autobiographical, as shown by the change of only two letters in the surname of his hero, and deals with a boyhood voyage to San Francisco, whaling adventures reminiscent of *Moby Dick*, fighting and gun-running in the Samoan civil war, and blackbirding in the Solomons. The novel includes an encounter with Captain "Bully" Hayes, the buccaneer with whom Becke sailed in his youth as supercargo. Becke's shrewdness as an amateur naturalist in the Pacific is shown in a number of volumes, such as *Wild Life in Southern Seas* (London: Unwin, 1897; New York: New Amsterdam Book Co., 1898) and *Notes from My South Sea Log* (London: T. Werner Laurie, 1905; Philadelphia: Lippincott,

Louis Becke, a biographer of Bully Hayes, as a successful author long after his two decades of wandering the Pacific islands.

1926). A criticobiographical study is *Louis Becke* by A. Grove Day in the Twayne World Authors Series, No. 9 (New York: Twayne, 1966), which includes a complete bibliography. *South Sea Supercargo* (Honolulu: University of Hawaii Press, 1967; Brisbane: Jacaranda Press, 1967), a collection of stories edited by A. Grove Day, features "Tom Denison", Becke's *alter ego*.

[69] SIR BASIL HOME THOMSON, K.C.B. *South Sea Yarns*. London: Blackwood, 1894.

A colonial administrator who later became director of intelligence at Scotland Yard wrote several books about the South Pacific.

Basil Thomson (1861–1939) was born at Queen's College, Oxford, son of the college provost, who afterwards became Archbishop of York. Basil was educated at Eton and Oxford, and began serving in the colonial corps for a decade in Fiji, Tonga (where he was prime minister of the kingdom), and New Guinea. Called to the London bar in 1896, he became governor successively of several prisons, and in 1913 was assistant commissioner of the Metropolitan Police. Through his leadership, almost all enemy agents in the British Isles were rounded up at the outbreak of World War I. Thomson resigned from Scotland Yard in 1931, and continued to publish books, particularly on crime and detection.

South Sea Yarns is a collection of short stories and sketches. Of particular interest are "The First Colonist", concerning the wild career of Charles Savage, who made himself master of Bau in Fiji until killed at the hill on Viti Levu in sight of Peter Dillon (see No. 43); and "The Coolie Princess", about a Chinese plantation worker at Fiji who refused to do any labor.

Other books by Thomson about the South Pacific are *Diversions of a Prime Minister* (London: Blackwood, 1894), concerning Tonga; *The Indiscretions of Lady Asenath* (London: A. D. Innes, 1898), a novel; *Savage Island: An Account of a Sojourn in Niué and Tonga* (London: J. Murray, 1902); and *The Fijians: A Study of the Decay of Custom* (London: W. Heinemann, 1908); see also No. 13 and No. 28.

[70] ROBERT LOUIS STEVENSON. *Island Nights' Entertainments.* London: Cassell, 1893. New York: Scribner, 1893.

Stevenson's name is inextricably associated with the South Seas, where he spent his last years and where he was buried.

Robert Louis Stevenson (1850–1894) was born in Edinburgh. He forsook the family profession of engineering in favor of literature. In San Francisco in 1888 he was able, by means of income from books like *Treasure Island* (1883) and *Kidnapped* (1886), to charter the yacht *Casco*, and set sail for the Pacific Islands. With him was his aged mother, his wife—the former Mrs. Frances (Fanny) Osbourne, whom he had married in California in 1879, and his stepson, Lloyd Osbourne.

The Stevensons cruised through the Marquesas Islands, the Tuamotus, the Society group, and Hawaii. They were welcomed everywhere, and everywhere "Louis" collected material for stories and articles.

During five months in 1889 the party was friendly with the reigning King Kalakaua and his sister, Liliuokalani, destined to be the last of the kingdom's rulers. Louis was also friendly with the Scottish merchant A. S. Cleghorn, who had married Princess Miriam Likelike and lived at Waikiki; to their daughter Kaiulani, who was leaving for Britain, he sent a parting verse beginning "Forth from her land to mine she goes . . ." At Waikiki he also wrote "The Song of Rahero" and "The Feast of Famine", based on native materials from the Marquesas and Tahiti. Stevenson toured the Kona region of the island of Hawaii and also Molokai, where he spent eight days at the leper settlement. There he collected information about the recently deceased Father Joseph Damien de Veuster, Belgian priest whom Stevenson afterward, in Sydney, Australia, fiercely defended in his "Open Letter to the Rev. Doctor Hyde" (1890).

The *Casco* having been sent back to California, the Stevensons later sailed in the schooner *Equator* to the Gilberts and Samoa, where R.L.S. was given the name of "Tusitala" or "teller of tales". He bought three hundred acres of land under Mount Vaea, high above the town of Apia on Upolu. In Australia, the family realized that Louis, a lifelong sufferer from tuberculosis, could stay alive only in a tropical climate. His wife arranged a cruise among the islands in a 600-ton trading steamer, the *Janet Nicol*. The party returned to Samoa in October, 1890, and moved into a cottage on their land, an estate named Vailima or Five Waters. The author varied writing with chopping undergrowth in the forest, despite his sickly frame.

During the *Equator* cruise, Stevenson had planned an ambitious volume on the Pacific. Its contents would be as outlined: Part I, "Of Schooners, Islands, and Maroons"; II, "The Marquesas"; III, "The Dangerous Archipelago" or Tuamotus; IV, "Tahiti"; V, "The Eight Islands" or Hawaii; VI, "The Gilberts"; and VII, Samoa". "If I can execute what is designed," he wrote, "there are few better books now extant on the globe." At least no writer, even of the epics, he added, had such rich material at hand. Parts II, III, and VI finally appeared in his volume *In the South Seas* (London: Chatto & Windus, 1900; New York: Scribner, 1896); some editions include a portion of Part V, concerning Hawaii. Parts I and IV were never written. The material gathered for the section on Samoa involved Stevenson deeply in the steamy arena of international island-grabbing and gunboat diplomacy, siding with the Samoans against the great powers. One result was the volume *A Footnote to History* (London: Cassell, 1892), with its famous description of the hurricane of 1889. Another result was that some Samoan political prisoners he had aided, when freed in September, 1894, hacked a road through the forest up to his mansion and christened it "Ala Loto Alofa", the Road of Loving Hearts.

Stevenson made a five-week return to Hawaii in 1893, where he found his royal friend Liliuokalani dethroned and a provisional government in power, led mainly by pro-American annexationists. Thereafter he remained in Samoa but continued, despite worsening health, to be active. He worked on many manuscripts, and even dictated his unfinished masterpiece, *Weir of Hermiston*. A sudden cerebral hemorrhage brought an end to his life in December, 1894. The Samoans carried his coffin to the summit of Vaea, where his tomb was inscribed with the words of his own verse, "Requiem".

Island Nights' Entertainments consists of three celebrated stories. "The Bottle Imp", set in the Hawaiian Islands and Tahiti, deals with the universal theme of magic wishes and their consequences.

The author called it "one of my best works, and ill to equal". "The Isle of Voices", set in Hawaii and an unnamed South Sea island, also involves the supernatural and Polynesian lore. "The Beach at Falesá", presumably located on a Samoan island and dealing with a white trader blighted by a tabu incited by a villainous competitor, is a novelette that perhaps shows Stevenson at his best in Pacific fiction. "It is the first realistic South Sea story," he wrote to his friend Sidney Colvin; "I mean with real South Sea character and details of life. . . . You will know more about the South Seas after you have read my little tale than if you had read a library." This story is the basis of a film treatment by the Welsh poet Dylan Thomas.

Stevenson, in collaboration with his stepson Lloyd Osbourne (see No. 73), wrote two novels of the Pacific. *The Wrecker* (London: Cassell, 1892) was inspired by accounts of the mysterious wreck of the bark *Wandering Minstrel* on Midway Island in 1888 (see No. 67). *The Ebb-Tide* (London: Heinemann, 1894; Chicago: Stone & Kimball, 1894) pictures not only the sea but the back streets of Papeete and Nouméa, haunts of sinister beachcombers.

Coming to the South Seas late in his life, R.L.S. nevertheless saw them with a clear eye. His attitude toward the Polynesians was always one of admiration and respect, though he sometimes looked upon them as a proud Highland chieftain might have looked on his faithful clansmen.

A number of sources are available on the Stevensons in the Pacific. The official *Life of Robert Louis Stevenson* is by his cousin, Sir Graham Balfour (London: Methuen, 1901; New York: Scribner, 1901). His *Letters to His Family and Friends*, 2 vol. (London: Methuen, 1899) were edited by Sidney Colvin. To these should be added *Vailima Letters to Sidney Colvin* (London: Methuen, 1895). Other references on the Pacific include Isobel (Osbourne) Strong and Lloyd Osbourne, *Memories of Vailima* (New York: Scribner, 1903); Arthur Johnstone, *Recollections of Robert Louis Stevenson in the Pacific* (London: Chatto & Windus, 1905); Harry Jay Moors, *With Stevenson in Samoa* (Boston: Small, Maynard, 1910); Richard Arnold Bermann, *Home from the Sea: Robert Louis Stevenson in Samoa*, translated by Elizabeth Reynolds Hapgood (Indianapolis, Ind.: Bobbs-Merrill, 1939); Sister Martha Mary McGaw, *Stevenson in Hawaii* (Honolulu: University of Hawaii

Press, 1950); J. C. Furnas, *Voyage to Windward* (London: Gollancz, 1950; New York: William Sloane Associates, 1951); and Joseph Waldo Ellison, *Tusitala of the South Seas; the Story of Robert Louis Stevenson's Life in the South Pacific* (New York: Hastings House, 1953).

[71] HENRY BROOKS ADAMS. *Memoirs of Arii Taimai o Marama of Eimeo, Teriirere of Tooaria, Teriinui of Tahiti, Tauraatua i Amo.* Paris: privately printed, 1901.

Historian and traveler, scion of the famed Adams family of New England, Henry Adams (1838–1918)—in company with the painter John Lafarge (see No. 72)—visited Hawaii, Samoa, Tahiti, Fiji, Australia, and the Netherlands East Indies. In Tahiti he talked for many hours with members of the Teva clan, especially with Hinari Salmon and her daughter Marau Taaroa, "the last Queen of Tahiti", who translated the family recollections. Marau Taaroa, whose father was an English merchant, Alexander Salmon, had been married to King Pomaré V but had divorced him because of his wayward life.

The first edition of this book, called *Memoirs of Marau Taaroa, Last Queen of Tahiti*, called "the rarest book on Tahiti", was privately printed in 1893. Only three copies are extant. The book was revised and privately published in Paris under the above title, but it is often called *Tahiti* from its half-title. The latter version is ostensibly the recollections of a noble lady, heroine of conciliation during the French conquest; her actions are given, supposedly in her own words, at the end of the book. The volume, however, is a thin mask for Adams the historian and collector of lore and legends of Tahiti, to which he added excerpts from the journals of voyagers such as James Cook and Samuel Wallis. It may also be an attempt to aggrandize the Teva clan over the Pomarés; see Robert Langdon, "A View on Ari'i Taimai's Memoirs", *Journal of Pacific History*, IV (1969), 162–65.

This lesser known book by the author of *Mont-Saint-Michel and Chartres* and *The Education of Henry Adams* is available as *Tahiti*, edited with an introduction by Robert E. Spiller (New York: Scholars' Facsmilies and Reprints, 1947). A more recent reprint, *Tahiti: Memoirs of Arii Taimai* (Ridgewood, N.J.: Gregg

Press, 1968), from the Paris edition, contains an introduction by Fred C. Sawyer. Other interesting observations by Adams on the South Seas are found in his *Letters, 1858–1891*, edited by Worthington Chauncey Ford (Boston and New York: Houghton, Mifflin, 1930).

[72] JOHN LA FARGE. *Reminiscences of the South Seas.* New York: Doubleday, Page & Co., 1912.

John La Farge (1835–1910), painter, writer, and artist in stained glass, was born in New York but was proud of his French ancestry (his father had served in the Napoleonic wars). He lived much of the time in Europe, but in 1890–91, in company with Henry Adams (see No. 71), voyaged to various parts of the Pacific. His travel letters, collected in this volume, equal his paintings in eloquence; the book includes forty-eight illustrations from paintings and drawings made during this period. On the Pacific journey, remarked Royal Cortissoz, La Farge "studied life with the directness of the explorer and with the more complex passion of the philosopher".

Descriptions in the volume reveal the painterly quality of La Farge's prose. His frequent use of color terms, as if language were mainly to be used as notes for future paintings, reminds us of a passage in *The Education of Henry Adams:* "In conversation La Farge's mind was opaline, with infinite shades and refractions of light, and with color toned down to the finest gradations."

[73] LLOYD OSBOURNE. *The Queen vs. Billy.* London: Heinemann, 1901. New York: Charles Scribner's Sons, 1900.

Lloyd Osbourne (1868–1947), son of Robert Louis Stevenson's wife, accompanied the Scottish author during his Pacific years (see No. 70) and collaborated with R.L.S. on two Pacific novels.

Lloyd was born in San Francisco and travelled with his mother and stepfather to Switzerland, Bournemouth, the Adirondacks in New York, and finally to Samoa. After being educated in private schools in England he studied engineering for two years at the University of Edinburgh. Following Stevenson's death in 1894, Osbourne served as American vice-consul at Samoa for three years. Later he went to New York and became fairly successful as an author of plays and fiction.

The Queen vs. Billy and *Wild Justice* (London: Heinemann, 1906; New York: Appleton-Century, 1906; reprinted with additional material, 1921) are two of Osbourne's best books. Both collect short stories with South Sea locales, which he knew well from his voyaging and his residence with the Stevensons. Apprenticeship with his famous stepfather prepared Osbourne for a happy literary career, and no anthology of Pacific fiction should leave him unrepresented.

[74] **JOSEPHINE H. NIAU.** *The Phantom Paradise: The Story of the Expedition of the Marquis de Rays.* Sydney: Angus and Robertson, 1936.

The gigantic swindle of the New Ireland colonization scheme perpetrated by the master criminal Charles-Mari-Bonaventure du Breil, Marquis de Rays, who called himself King Charles I of Nouvelle France, is told in this book by the daughter of one of the survivors.

Four successive shiploads of hopeful emigrants, departing from Europe in the late 1870s, were dumped on the most inhospitable shores of grim Melanesia, on a disease-ridden beach surrounded by jungle and cannibals. Their dreams of living in luxury as plantation owners in a new Eden were shattered by horrifying reality and sudden death for many, while their "king" stayed behind and squandered their mulcted millions.

Miss Niau tells the story in a personalized, journalistic style. The chain of events is also narrated in *Rascals in Paradise* (London: Secker & Warburg, 1957; New York: Random House, 1957, Chapter II) by James A. Michener and A. Grove Day. One of Alphonse Daudet's most bitter books, *Port-Tarascon* (Boston: Little, Brown, 1900, translated by Katherine P. Wormeley) satirizes this epic of folly as one of the adventures of Tartarin the Gascon.

[75] PAUL GAUGUIN. *Noa Noa: Voyage to Tahiti.* Translated from the French by Jonathan Griffin. Oxford: Bruno Cassirer, 1961.

Eugène Henri Paul Gauguin (1848–1903), a French artist born in Paris, is best known for his paintings of the South Seas. He spent part of his childhood in Peru, and after an education at the lycée at Orleans served for several years as a sailor in the merchant marine and the French Navy. He began in 1875 to paint in his spare time, and five years later, giving up his post as assistant to a stockbroker, he separated from his Danish wife and five children and devoted himself entirely to art. After several bitter years, he obtained some money by selling pictures at auction and in 1891 sailed for Tahiti. There he found the colorful scenes and "primitive" people he needed as subjects for his greatest work, as well as a simple mode of life that gave him freedom and pleasure. After another trip to Europe, he settled in the South Seas for good. His last two years were spent on the island of Hiva Oa in the Marquesas group, poor and in wretched health, but still painting brilliantly. A few years after his death, his reputation as an artist rose rapidly and the islands were searched for any scrap of his work that chanced to survive. W. Somerset Maugham (see No. 83) based a novel, *The Moon and Sixpence* (1919), upon Gauguin's life.

The title of Gauguin's only book, *Noa Noa*, comes from a common Tahitian adjective meaning "fragrant"; the noun "island" is understood. It suggests the Polynesian paradise. No edition offers exactly what Gauguin had in mind when in Paris in 1894, desiring to make some much needed money, he decided to write a book about his Tahiti adventures, in the hope of rivalling the best-selling *The Marriage of Loti* (see No. 63). He wanted the book also to explain his artistic theories, and therefore it should be illustrated with some of his pictures. The ten woodcuts he made for it have been considered his greatest prints.

Realizing the difficulties of authorship, Gauguin enlisted his journalist friend Charles Morice as collaborator, who would present some of the material in verse. Morice procrastinated in writing his share, and when Gauguin returned to the South Seas in 1895 he took with him, as a precaution, a copy of his own

Gauguin's portrait of Teha'amana (called Tehura in *Noa Noa*), who lived with the artist in Tahiti.

manuscript. A version of *Noa Noa*, with the poems of Morice, was first published in *La Revue Blanche* in Paris (October 15 and November 15, 1897). The book did not appear until 1901, without illustrations.

Current translations are based on *Noanoa: Voyage à Tahiti* (Stockholm: Jan Förlag, 1947), a facsimile edition of Gauguin's manuscript, with colored illustrations, some of them added later. According to Bengt Danielsson (see No. 76, 244), the manuscript taken to Tahiti, incomplete and amplified, is the one usually reprinted, whereas the neglected edition of 1901, with Morice's introduction and verses, along with Gauguin's ten woodcuts, "comes closest to Gauguin's original conception of the book".

The style of the Gauguin manuscript is overblown and fragmentary. The false impression is given that life in Tahiti—except for the town of Papeete—was still idyllic and primitive in the 1890s. It is impossible to believe, moreover, that Gauguin's thirteen-year-old mistress "Tehura" (Teha'amana) knew anything about the ancient gods of Polynesia. Gauguin presents a delectable view that was as far from his rather miserable existence as his paintings are from photographs.

[76] **BENGT DANIELSSON.** *Gauguin in the South Seas.* Translated from the Swedish by Reginald Spink. London: George Allen & Unwin, 1965. New York: Doubleday, 1966.

All other books discussing Paul Gauguin's South Sea years (see No. 75) are made obsolete by Bengt Danielsson's charming and factual volume, illustrated with old and modern photographs as well as reproductions of many of the French painter's works. The author is the only biographer of Gauguin who lived in the South Pacific.

Danielsson, born in Sweden in 1921, spent nineteen years in French Oceania. A social anthropologist with three degrees from the University of Uppsala, he spent much of his spare time building this chronicle of Gauguin's life and the places where he lived in the South Seas. Dr. Danielsson talked to more than a hundred persons whose testimony might prove valuable, and supplemented oral tradition by study of many previously unused documents, such as records in the government archives at Papeete, local newspapers, missionary journals published in France, travel descriptions by visitors, and a number of letters to Gauguin and from him. In addition to providing the most accurate account of the painter's ten years in the South Seas and describing the conditions in French Oceania at the time, Danielsson aimed "to try to understand and explain Gauguin's actions, reactions, difficulties, griefs, and triumphs, as the consequences of the interplay of a unique personality and a unique local environment".

A skilled writer, Danielsson handles a style that can be ironic as well as exotic. His description, for instance, of the various classes living in Papeete when Gauguin arrived includes the intrigues and feuds of official circles: "The commonest causes of these disputes were potatoes and native girls. The former article was chronically in short supply as it had to be imported, and soon went bad on the long voyage out. Since no official's wife could ever contemplate the idea of profaning the sacred traditions of the French *cuisine* by replacing *pommes frites* with yams, breadfruits, sweet potatoes, or any of the other delicious Tahitian vegetables, the battle for the few boxes of potatoes which at long intervals arrived unspoilt was bitter and ruthless. The problem of the native girls was exactly the opposite: they were too plentiful, and the officials were therefore inclined to turn to their arms for comfort and relaxation from the frustrating potato wars" (69).

Danielsson was a member of the crew of the *Kon-Tiki* (see No. 98), which broke up on Raroia in the Tuamotu archipelago. He liked this island so greatly that he returned with his wife to spend a year there—an adventure described in his book *The Happy Island* (London: George Allen & Unwin, 1952). Other volumes for the general reader include: *Love in the South Seas* (London: George Allan & Unwin, 1956; New York, Reynal, 1956); *Forgotten Islands of the South Seas* (London: George Allan & Unwin, 1957); *From Raft to Raft* (London: George Allan & Unwin, 1960; New York: Doubleday, 1960), an account of the voyages of Eric de Bisschop; and *What Happened on the "Bounty"* (London: George Allen & Unwin, 1962; New York: Rand McNally, 1964).

[77] C. A. W. MONCKTON. *Taming New Guinea: Some Experiences of a New Guinea Resident Magistrate.* London: John Lane, 1921. New York: Dodd, Mead, 1922.

Of the many books of reminiscence about the vast island of New Guinea, none are better informed or more engrossing than those of Magistrate Monckton.

Charles Arthur Whitmore Monckton (1872–1936) was born in New Zealand and educated at Wanganui College. As a young man he went to New Guinea, where for a time he engaged in pearl fishing and prospecting for gold. In 1898 he was appointed resident magistrate for the unadministered district of northeastern New Guinea, charged with enforcing British law and justice among natives bent on following ancient tribal customs despite the newly organized government. For nine years Monckton, with his native constabulary and occasional white assistants, hunted murderers, protected miners and traders, outwitted sorcerers, led expeditions against raiding tribes, and performed the many other dangerous duties required by his position. Sent on several missions into the interior, he gathered information on previously unknown native tribes and explored much of the mountainous, almost impenetrable territory, including the treacherous Wasia River and the ranges that lie between Kaiser Wilhelm Land and the Gulf of Papua. He resigned from the government service in 1907 and went to England; during World War I he served as a captain in the British army.

Taming New Guinea covers Monckton's activities up to 1903, ending with the expedition over the Hydrographer's Range. The sequel is *Further Adventures of a New Guinea Resident Magistrate* (London: John Lane, 1922; *Last Days in New Guinea*, New York: Dodd, Mead, 1922). Random reminiscences are found in *New Guinea Recollections* (London: John Lane, 1934). Monckton is a good yarn spinner with a sharp eye for details.

[78] GEORGE CALDERON. *Tahiti.* London: Grant Richards, 1921. New York: Harcourt, Brace, 1922.

Of the many books of reminiscences by sojourners in Tahiti, none is more frank and uniquely personal than that by George Calderon.

Calderon went to Rugby in the 1880s, where he mastered several languages, wrote one-act dramas, and played the piano. He visited Tahiti in 1906, and his interest was so intense that on his return to England he spent some years of laborious research into the history of the European influences to which the islanders had been exposed. Not until the winter before the outbreak of World War I did he begin to write his book. In spite of his age and indifferent health, he volunteered for service, and vanished into the smoke of battle at Gallipoli on June 4, 1915.

Tahiti was put together by Calderon's widow Katharine from manuscripts and notes, but as she says, "There has been no smoothing or polishing by any hand but his own." The author's candor is clear throughout, and is reinforced by this note on one of his manuscripts: "Everything set down in this book is true. I have thought it important, for a right understanding of individual lives, and thereby a conglomeration of detail, to give a picture of the whole, to put down personal details which I have been told or found out about people. The only untruth is that I have sufficiently disguised the personality of those of whom they are told, so that no one should recognize them."

Calderon was an energetic observer of Tahiti in 1906; he went everywhere and talked to everyone. He enjoyed chatting with the *bayadères,* as he called the Tahitian girl entertainers. He met Ernest Darling, the "nature man" who had fled from California to find brimming health in the hills of Tahiti. George visited Loti's pool and strolled among the villages, collecting legends. His book is illustrated by fifty pencil sketches by the author.

Calderon was a personality as well as a writer. A former schoolmaster at Rugby, G. F. Bradby, wrote of him: "He was the most original man I have ever known. . . . It was all a part, I think, of his intense mental honesty. . . . He knew as well as anybody that no one is gifted with perfect vision; his might fail him, but he would never pretend that he saw facts otherwise than as he saw them, and, regardless of consequences to himself, he stuck to his vision of 'things as they are', with dogged, almost obstinate honesty. And from first to last there was always in him something of the knight-errant; but never before have knight-errants been so witty as he was." Readers are fortunate that such a man was able to observe and report on Tahiti in the early part of our century.

[79] JACK LONDON. *The Cruise of the "Snark"*. London: Mills & Boon, 1913. New York: Harper, 1908.

Jack London (1876–1916), after an adventurous youth as oyster pirate in San Francisco Bay, sailor on a sealing ship, hobo, student for one semester at the University of California, and prospector in the Alaskan gold rush, taught himself to write, and eventually became before his death the best known, highest paid, and most popular writer in the world.

Jack London and his "mate," Charmian, plan their *Snark* cruising through the South Seas.

The idea of cruising around the world on a sailing vessel designed by himself came to Jack London while chatting around a swimming pool at Glen Ellen, California, in 1905. He wished to emulate Captain Joshua Slocum's circumnavigating exploits, and hoped that the voyage could be financed by writing magazine articles along the way. The *Snark* turned out to be a boojum. Everything went wrong that could go wrong, as London shows in describing his "inconceivable and monstrous" adventures in building the craft and making a dangerous traverse to Honolulu in 1907. This was the beginning of a two-year cruise in the South Seas, including the Marquesas, the Society group, Samoa, Fiji, the Solomons, and the New Hebrides. The cruise ended when London became seriously ill from an affliction that he believed came from the continuous exposure of a blond skin to tropical sunlight; it was more likely pellagra.

A number of other volumes by London resulted from his cruise. These include *Adventure* (London: Mills, 1911; New York, Macmillan, 1911), *South Sea Tales* (same), and *A Son of the Sun* (London: Mills, n.d.; New York: Doubleday, Page, 1912). Also to be mentioned are two "dog stories" set mainly in the New Hebrides, *Jerry of the Islands* (London: Mills, 1917; New York, Macmillan, 1917) and *Michael, Brother of Jerry* (same). An account of the voyage by London's wife Charmian is *The Log of the "Snark"* (London and New York: Macmillan, 1915). Charmian also published *The Book of Jack London* (New York: Century, 1921) and his daughter Joan London wrote *Jack London and His Times* (New York: Doubleday, Doran, 1934). A recent account of the Londons in the Pacific is *Jack London in the South Seas* (New York: Four Winds Press, 1970) by A. Grove Day.

[80] SYDNEY W. POWELL. *A South Sea Diary.* London: Gollancz, 1942.

An Englishman went to French Oceania before World War I, married a Tahitian girl, and worked for many months in the islands as planter and trader.

Sydney Walter Powell was born in London in 1878. After a high-school education he went into the civil service of Natal and then enlisted during the South African War. Afterwards he spent two years in Matabeleland as a trooper in the British South Africa Police. He then went "bushwhacking" in Australia and served in the Royal Australian Artillery. From New Zealand he went to Tahiti. His diary, from February 9, 1912, to April 27, 1913, is a realistic presentation of a white man's existence, as well as the record of an ill-fated love. At the outbreak of World War I, he was chopping scrub in the "back-blocks" of New South Wales, but by dint of hard traveling he arrived in Sydney in time to join the First Division of the Australian Imperial Force. He took part in the Anzac landing at Gallipoli. Invalided with wounds, he returned to the South Seas and Australia, but finally went home to England and began a writing career.

At Tahiti, Powell had married an attractive girl, Tehiva, and bought a small coconut plantation where they lived in idyllic happiness. Tehiva loved to go fishing, and Sydney wandered in the high woods, hunting rare herbs. Then the Englishman was stricken with the dread disease of elephantiasis and a swollen leg. He was ordered by his doctor to travel at least five hundred miles from Tahiti and to stay away for an entire year. Fortunately he got the job of plantation manager on the island of Makemo in the Tuamotu or Low Archipelago. His employer, an American, well described the disadvantages of atoll life for a "civilized" man: "Day after day, week after week, month after month. And the plantation's a good way from the settlement—about fourteen miles down the lagoon. You've got the coconut trees, the sea and the lagoon, and that's all there is—except bush at each end of the plantation. You can run about the lagoon in your cutter, but there's not much else you can do. There are no birds but sea birds, no animals. Except dogs and domestic pigs there isn't a four-legged creature on the island. You've no neighbors, not even brown ones. There are two other white men on the atoll, one of them our trader, but they're both up at the settlement. You see a schooner occasionally, but most of them pass you. What does your girl think about it?"

Fortunately, Tehiva agreed, and the Powells began to see the Tuamotus—Makatéa, Anaa, Hao. Sydney did well managing the plantation on Makemo, and later was assigned to supervise thirty-eight divers during the pearl-shell season on Hikueru, as well as to run the store and buy copra. But Tehiva developed tuberculosis, and Powell was forced to take her back to Papeete for treatment. His ailment was cured for ever, but when they returned to their old plantation, Tehiva was not sufficiently careful. One day, while she drifted alone in a canoe, a sudden squall capsized the frail craft and she tried to haul it ashore. That night she had a hemorrhage and died at once. Powell could not bear to remain at Tahiti and soon departed for Australia.

Powell's other books are not distinguished. *Adventures of a Wanderer* (London: Cape, 1928) is a fairly readable autobiography. *Tales from Tahiti* (London: E. Benn, 1928) consists of short stories. Several novels, such as *South Sea Fortune* (London: Macdonald, 1944), are routine local color. His *Diary*, however, is a document that pulses with life. Although Powell was not a romantic, a vision of peace and beauty is evoked by his candid account of his South Sea adventures.

[81] "ASTERISK" [ROBERT JAMES FLETCHER]. *Isles of Illusion: Letters from the South Seas.* Edited by Bohun Lynch. London: Constable, 1925. New York: Small, Maynard, 1923.

A restless young English schoolmaster, having read too much Stevenson, worked his way via South America to dwell in the legendary South Seas. He landed in what is probably the most uncomfortable group of islands in the Pacific, the New Hebrides, where he spent seven-and-a-half years before escaping from a painful and often dangerous existence as a plantation manager. He then worked for six months on an island in French Polynesia, and after a sojourn in Tahiti disappeared from our ken.

Fletcher's semi-autobiographical novel, *Gone Native: A Tale of the South Seas* (London: Constable, 1924), lacks the strength of the letters, written to an Oxford classmate and published under the pseudonym of "Asterisk". These letters, written between 1912 and 1920, will remain as a testament of the clash between the temperament of a cultured dreamer and the inevitable disenchantments of his grim life.

Fletcher might have posed for the portrait of Crichton in

James Norman Hall's "The Forgotten One", although this short story was historically modeled on another real person, Arthur Cridland, a civilized expatriate who also craved solitude as if it were a drug. "I have often wondered," wrote Hall in an appreciative essay concerning Fletcher—"A Happy Hedonist" (in *The Forgotten One*, Boston: Little, Brown, 1952, 102–130)—"why it is that tropical solitude seems harder to bear than that of the unfrequented places of the north. A gray, misty, northern sea with never a sail on it is nothing like so lonely as a tropical sea, bright and blue and sparkling in the afternoon sunshine." Fletcher was probably a man who would not have been happy anywhere, but this frank record of disillusion is still a strong antidote for those who feel that freedom may be found in far Melanesia.

[82] SIR ARTHUR GRIMBLE. *A Pattern of Islands.* London: John Murray, 1952. American title, *We Chose the Islands.* New York: William Morrow, 1952.

One cannot nowadays think of the Gilbert Islanders without thinking of Arthur Grimble (1888–1956), who after retirement wrote his recollections of nineteen years in those islands and began reading them over the British Broadcasting network. Later these were published in two highly successful books; the sequel was called *Return to the Islands* (London: John Murray; New York: William Morrow, 1957).

With a degree from Cambridge University and further education in France and Germany, Grimble joined the British Colonial Service at the age of twenty-six and was posted to the Gilbert and Ellice Islands Protectorate. There he remained from 1914 until 1933, first as cadet and then, joined by his family and having demonstrated his competence by mastering the Gilbertese language and penetrating the modes of thought of these Polynesians, as Resident Commissioner, chief administrator of the group. After leaving the Pacific, he acted as governor of the Seychelles Islands, was knighted in 1938, and ended his colonial career with a post in the Windward Islands.

Grimble's apparently rambling chapters often form complete tales. His style is light and sometimes humorous. He does, however, reveal a deep understanding of the Gilbertese modes of reasoning and his appreciation of their customs and folklore; in several yarns he apparently shares their belief in the existence of ghosts.

[83] W. SOMERSET MAUGHAM. *The Trembling of a Leaf.* New York: George H. Doran Company. London: W. Heinemann, 1921.

Maugham (1874–1965), noted English novelist, playwright, and author of short stories, spent several months in the Pacific in 1916 and 1917 during an interlude in his service in British intelligence in World War I. He had wanted to go to the South Seas, he said, "ever since as a youth I had read *The Ebb-Tide* and *The Wrecker*", by Stevenson, as well as the writings of Melville and Loti.

Maugham's keen observation and his narrative art are at their height in a sheaf of stories that were not published until several years later. All those dealing with the Pacific Islands—"Mackintosh", "The Fall of Edward Barnard", "Red", "The Pool", "Honolulu", and "Rain"—were collected in *The Trembling of a Leaf.* Several of these were made into motion pictures; "Rain" was a successful stage play and three film versions have appeared.

The Moon and Sixpence (London: Heinemann, 1919; New York: George H. Doran, 1919), Maugham's novel about the life of a British counterpart of Paul Gauguin, has only the last few chapters set in the South Seas.

An illustrated account of Maugham in the Pacific appears in *The Two Worlds of Somerset Maugham* (Los Angeles: Sherbourne Press, 1965) by Wilmon Menard.

[84] FREDERICK O'BRIEN. *White Shadows in the South Seas.* New York: Century, 1919.

After the disillusion of World War I, many Americans yearned to escape their mundane occupations and find an Eden in the tropics. One man who did escape and arouse others to seek the South Seas was Frederick O'Brien, then nearing the age of fifty. His writings, which evoke a nostalgia among those who devoured them for the first time in the 1920s, have well withstood the years since then. The first of his books, and still the best remembered, is *White Shadows in the South Seas*, an account of a year spent in the Marquesas group.

"It is for those who stay at home yet dream of foreign places that I have written this book," says O'Brien, "a record of one happy year spent among the simple, friendly cannibals of Atuona Valley, on the island of Hiva Oa in the Marquesas." After leaving Papeete on the schooner *Fetia Taiao* (Morning Star), O'Brien spent thirty-seven days at sea before sighting the Marquesas. He went ashore, at once hired a thirteen-year-old valet named Nakohu or "Exploding Eggs", and set up housekeeping in Atuona Valley, capital of "the man-eating isle of Hiva Oa". His year in the Marquesas enabled him to converse with the native people, remnants of proud Polynesian tribes, and to relate adventures by himself and his friends. O'Brien visited the site of Paul Gauguin's last home (see No. 75) but failed to discover his grave. Later he journeyed to the island of Nuku Hiva and sojourned in Melville's valley of Taipi (see No. 51), where O'Brien heard the tale of the captain of an American ocean liner, who had returned to seek his Marquesan sweetheart and found only a score of people in the valley where the natives once had happily thronged.

O'Brien gives accounts of native customs and superstitions. Although he says he traveled light, "without the heavy baggage of the ponderous-minded scholar", he draws upon ethnological records and accounts of earlier visitors to the Marquesas.

O'Brien (1869–1932) followed his first success with *Mystic Isles of the South Seas* (London: Hodder & Stoughton, 1921; New York: Century, 1921), with its setting mainly in Tahiti, and *Atolls of the Sun* (London: Hodder & Stoughton, 1922; New York: Century, 1922), dealing with the Tuamotu Archipelago and the Marquesas.

[85] **WILLOWDEAN C. HANDY.** *Forever the Land of Men: An Account of a Visit to the Marquesas Islands.* New York: Dodd, Mead, 1965.

The name of the Marquesan Archipelago in the language of the people is Fenua Enata, The Land of Men. Mrs. Handy's book is an excellent tale by a member of a scientific expedition to the

Design of a tortoise-shell crown. The incised design portrays the ceremony of carrying the first-born of the chief on the head and shoulders of his mother's brother.

Marquesas, and the best book revealing the lives of women in these scattered, still primitive islands.

Willowdean Chatterton Handy (1889–1965), born in Louisville, Kentucky, earned a Ph.B. degree at the University of Chicago in 1909. She attended the Radcliffe graduate school in 1915–1917, and married Edward S. Craighill Handy in 1918. With her husband, who became ethnologist of the Bayard Dominick Expedition of the Bernice P. Bishop Museum of Honolulu during 1920 and 1921, she went to the Marquesas as a volunteer. It was soon discovered that the ancient Marquesan art of tattooing could not be recorded by means of photographs, and Mrs. Handy was enlisted to sketch these figures for scientific study. Her pen-and-ink drawings are today the main source of knowledge concerning these important designs. In order to obtain rapport with the many people whose decorations she copied, she taught herself a number of string figures or "cat's cradles", along with the stories that went with each figure.

"Anthropologists will find the book of considerable interest," states Dr. Robert C. Suggs, prominent researcher in Marquesan ethnology, "because it presents the hitherto unavailable human dimensions of the activities of this highly successful expedition.... One also gets a good glimpse of field work and theory in an important period of Polynesian anthropological investigation." Mrs. Handy draws upon various earlier printed sources on Marquesan life. Above all, *Forever the Land of Men* is a warm personal story of a happy relationship between twentieth-century scientists and a Polynesian people with an undeservedly tragic history.

[86] ROBERT DEAN FRISBIE. *The Book of Puka-Puka.* London and New York: Century, 1929.

Frisbie (1896–1948), born in Cleveland, Ohio, went to the South Seas after World War I ostensibly to treat his tuberculosis, but actually because he was an idealist who dreamed of setting up as owner of a wandering trading schooner and earning other money by writing. After "going native" for several years near Papeete he began twelve years of drifting about the islands. "Ropati", as he was called, in 1924 became a resident trader on Puka-Puka or Danger Island in the northern Cook Group. He stayed for four years, married twice, and by his second wife Nga had five children. He had always been an omnivorous reader. In the midst of an active life he wrote his first and best book, undoubtedly one of the most delightful accounts of a white man living on a distant atoll.

His wanderings continued after 1928, marked by the death of his wife and the burden of rearing a large, motherless family. Hearing of the outbreak of World War II, he left with his family with the intention of enlisting. During a hurricane on Suvarov or Suwarrow Island, where they were detained in February, 1942, Frisbie lost most of his possessions, including manuscripts and notes. His health, complicated by filariasis and bouts of alcoholism, was never good. Nevertheless, he continued to publish, through hard work and despite many rejections, a number of volumes of interest, although his powers were declining. These are *My Tahiti* (Boston: Little, Brown, 1937); *Mr. Moonlight's Island* (New York: Farrar & Rinehart, 1939); *Island of Desire* (New York: Doubleday, Doran, 1944); *Amaru* (same, 1945); and *Dawn Sails North* (New York: Doubleday, 1949). He also aided his daughter Florence (whom he had nicknamed "Whiskey Johnny") to write *Miss Ulysses from Puka-Puka: the Autobiography of a South Sea Trader's Daughter* (New York: Macmillan, 1948). "Johnny" later published an account of her family in *The Frisbies of the South Seas* (New York: Doubleday, 1959).

Frisbie was a friend of James Norman Hall for twenty-eight years, but they seldom saw each other and hence wrote many letters; some are quoted in Hall's warmly appreciative essay, "Frisbie of Danger Island", in *The Forgotten One* (Boston: Little, Brown, 1952, 154–246).

[87] MARGARET MEAD. *Coming of Age in Samoa.* New York: William Morrow, 1928.

A field study designed to answer the question, "Are the disturbances which vex our [Occidental] adolescents due to the nature of adolescence itself or to the civilization?", resulted in a popular account of Samoan life on a distant island, an account which is still pertinent.

Miss Mead spent nine months in American Samoa, mainly on the little island of Tau in the Manua group east of Pago Pago. She concentrated on knowing all the girls of three coastal villages, speaking their language and sharing their feelings. Their experiences revealed a marked gap between the strains of American adolescence and the comparative tranquility of the islanders. "Familiarity with sex, and the recognition of a need of a technique to deal with sex as an art, have produced a scheme of personal relations in which there are no neurotic pictures, no frigidity, no impotence, except as the temporary result of severe illness, and the capacity for intercourse only once in a night is counted as senility." One of Miss Mead's conclusions is: "With the exception of [a few cases], adolescence represented no period of crisis or stress, but was instead an orderly developing of a set of slowly maturing interests and activities. The girls' minds were perplexed by no conflicts, troubled by no philosophical queries, beset by no remote ambitions. To live as a girl with many lovers as long as possible and then to marry in one's own village, near one's own relatives, and to have many children, these were uniform and satisfying ambitions."

While it is unlikely that the people of Manua are still unspoiled more than forty years later, Miss Mead's descriptions of their "primitive" life might continue, in the words of Franz Boas, to "confirm the suspicion long held by anthropologists, that much of what we ascribe to human nature is no more than a reaction to the restraints put upon us by our civilization".

Dr. Margaret Mead has devoted her career to energetic revelations of the relationships between psychology and culture. Born in Philadelphia, Pennsylvania, in 1901, she attended De Pauw University and Barnard College. Her Samoan study was used as a dissertation for a Doctor of Philosophy degree at Columbia University in 1929. She became assistant curator of ethnology at the American Museum of Natural History in New York City in 1926 and progressed to the post of curator of ethnology in 1964. She took part in expeditions to the Admiralty Islands, Bali, and New Guinea; the last of these resulted in another Pacific classic, *Growing Up in New Guinea* (London: Routledge, 1931;

New York: Morrow, 1930). Dr. Mead has written or edited a number of other books in anthropology and psychology, and is a member of many professional societies.

[88] ROBERT LEE ESKRIDGE. *Manga Reva: the Forgotten Islands.* Indianapolis, Ind. Bobbs-Merrill, 1931.

An American painter was charmed by the life of the people of the Gambier group in French Oceania, and collected many stories from their past.

Born in 1891, Robert Lee Eskridge wandered around the world as an artist, and spent much time in Hawaii and the South Seas. His book, illustrated with drawings by the author, contains reflections on the "Lost Continent" theory in the Pacific, tales of ghosts and magic, and personal experiences with the isolated folk of the cannibal Gambiers. This group was first found by Captain James Wilson of the *Duff* (see No. 34), who named the cluster for Admiral James Gambier and gave to the highest peak the name of Mount Duff.

Eskridge's Chapter 4, "Honoré Laval, the Mad Priest", is acknowledged as a main source for an historical novel, Garland Roark's *The Witch of Manga Reva* (New York: Doubleday, 1962). Laval, who wrote in French an archeological account of Mangareva, went in 1834 with Father Caret as a missionary of the Society of Picpus to become the apostle of this island. Laval obtained dominance over the chief, the fifteenth of his line, and began a compulsive building program that lasted almost forty years. A native police force was organized which enforced Laval's dictates. People were hauled from neighboring islands to slave at cutting stone blocks and erecting a spreading, 3,400-seat cathedral, churches, a monastery, and a nunnery (in which were immured gay Polynesian maidens forcibly enlisted into convent life). As the buildings spread, the people died. Finally a visit from his bishop put an end to Laval's reign in 1871, and the jungle began reclaiming his monuments. Laval died at Tahiti in 1880 and the Gambiers were annexed by France the following year.

[89] EARL SCHENCK. *Come Unto These Yellow Sands.* Indianapolis, Ind.: Bobbs-Merrill, 1940.

Born with a craving for the primitive life, Earl Schenck in college enjoyed studying anthropology and running cross-country, a sport that built up stamina for later years. He was still a boy when he played the lead in a Broadway drama, and later traveled with stock companies to many locations. As a film actor, he continued his search for isolated beaches near Hollywood. Stricken with eye trouble caused by studio lights, he continued acting in outdoor pageants in national parks. Half blind, hardly able to sign the contract for his last motion picture, he decided to take ship for Hawaii, where he had heard he might find peace in the isolated valley of Kalalau.

Schenck stayed in Hawaii for five years, becoming involved in celebrating the Captain Cook Sesquicentennial in 1928 and in taking part in other pageantry. When film companies began coming to Hawaii, he was swept up in directing and producing; Hollywood was following him across the sea. After he produced a play for a colony of Samoans at Laie, he realized that his life in the suburb of Kahala was not to be preferred to the quest for the real South Seas. He sold his house in 1933 and departed for Samoa.

Come Unto These Yellow Sands is a series of chapters on the author's wanderings in the South Pacific. After dwelling in American Samoa, he moved on to Fiji, New Zealand, Tahiti, and the Tuamotus. Felled by a fever supposedly caused by island ghosts on Vahitahi, he was rescued by the schooner *Moana* and convalesced at Tahiti. Lazy days went by, the world forgotten by the shore at Punaauia or among ancient tombs in the hills. When at last Schenck fell in love and took a steamer heading for the Panama Canal and the United States, he realized that fourteen years of his life had passed by, as if in a dream, among the islands of the Pacific.

Schenck's book is illustrated with drawings by the author. He also wrote *Lean With the Wind* (London: T. Werner Laurie, 1945; New York: Whittlesey House, 1945), a novel with a Tahiti setting.

[90] ROBERT GIBBINGS. *Over the Reefs.* London: Dent, 1948. New York: Dutton, 1949.

Robert Gibbings (1889–1958), Irish naturalist and artist, spent some time visiting the South Seas in the 1930s. His best book is *Over the Reefs*, excellently illustrated by the author.

This travel narrative opens in Tonga but soon passes to Samoa, a region that claims most of the book. Gibbings also visited the Tokelau group, the Cook Islands, Manihiki, Penrhyn and Tahiti. Gibbings had a keen draftsman's eye and a realistic style. He sought not the South Sea *mirage* but the everyday incidents. His wood engravings are as revealing as his text.

Other Pacific Islands volumes by Gibbings include *The Seventh Man: a True Cannibal Tale of the South Sea Islands* (London: Golden Cockerel Press, 1930; New York: Houghton, Mifflin, 1930) and *Iorana: A Tahitian Journal* (London: Duckworth, 1932; New York, Houghton, Mifflin, 1932). Pacific books he illustrated include William Bligh's *The Voyage of the "Bounty's" Launch* (London: Golden Cockerel Press, 1934); Owen Chase's *Narratives of the Wreck of the "Essex"* (London: Golden Cockerel Press, 1935); *Journal of James Morrison, Boatswain's Mate of the "Bounty"* . . . (London: Golden Cockerel Press, 1935); and John Fisher's *The Midmost Waters* (London: Naldrett Press, 1952).

[91] CLIFFORD GESSLER. *The Dangerous Islands.* London: M. Joseph, 1937. *Road My Body Goes.* New York: John Day, 1937.

Journalist and poet, Clifford Gessler joined a scientific expedition and spent many months ranging the Tuamotu or Dangerous Archipelago. His adventures are warmly narrated in two books that show the closeness with which a sympathetic *popaa* or white stranger can join in the life of scattered atoll dwellers.

Gessler, born in 1893, in Milton Junction, Wisconsin, obtained an M.A. degree at the University of Wisconsin and for a while taught in a high school. News reporting qualified him for a post in Honolulu, where from 1924 to 1934 he was telegraph and literary editor of the *Star-Bulletin*. Feeling the need of a change, he accepted an invitation to join the Mangarevan Expedition of the Bernice P. Bishop Museum of Honolulu, and in 1934 sailed to the Tuamotu group on the 90-foot sampan *Islander*. After his rambles in the South Pacific he became a magazine writer and a member of the staff of the Oakland, California, *Tribune*. A rare volume is *The Reasonable Life: Some Aspects of Polynesian Life* (New York: John Day, 1950). His collected verses are found in *Kanaka Moon* (New York: Dodd, Mead & Co., 1929) and *Tropic Earth* (Reno, Nev.: Wagon and Star, 1944). He also published two prose volumes about Hawaii.

The Dangerous Islands (American title, *Road My Body Goes*) tells mainly of Gessler's stay on the atoll of Napuka, which with its neighbor Tepoto form the northernmost of the Tuamotu Islands. He and Kenneth P. Emory ("Keneti"), then a Museum ethnologist and today the dean of Pacific archeologists, were the only outsiders on Napuka (the place of the *puka* tree) from May 15 to July 29, 1934. At one time Gessler nearly died of blood poisoning, far from a doctor. He describes amusingly the life led by these two "heaven breakers", and in an appendix gives valuable advice to those who believe that a Westerner can enjoy a paradisiacal existence if he manages to reach a Pacific atoll; the drawbacks are many, especially in French Oceania, even if one picks up a smattering of the local language. The book includes translations of several songs and a note on Tuamotuan literature.

Gessler went on the cutter *Tiare Tahiti*, by way of Vahitahi and several other islands, to Papeete, where he spent some time as a penniless beachcomber. His later adventures, wandering in the Tuamotu, Austral, and Society groups, are told in *The Leaning Wind* (London and New York: D. Appleton-Century, 1943).

[92] ERIC A. FELDT. *The Coast Watchers*. London and New York: Oxford University Press, 1946. Sydney: Angus & Robertson, 1967.

"They gained intelligence and relayed it by radio, guiding attacks on Jap planes and shipping; secretly evacuated civilians from behind enemy lines; rescued and helped evacuate allied airmen;

and, as the Japanese were being driven out, organized guerrilla warfare." Thus General Douglas MacArthur, Supreme Commander of the Allied Powers in World War II in the Pacific, paid tribute to the "coast watchers". And Admiral William A. Halsey declared: "The intelligence signalled from Bougainville by Read and Mason saved Guadalcanal, and Guadalcanal saved the South Pacific."

Read and Mason were only two of the scattered, volunteer band of devoted watchers organized under "Operation Ferdinand". The name was chosen to remind the men that, like Munro Leaf's bull, they were to sit quietly and gather information, not fighting unless they were stung.

The origin of coast watching in northern Australia and the islands beyond goes back to the end of World War I, when people living in strategic places were asked to report unusual activity on the exposed shorelines. In September, 1939, when Australia entered World War II, Eric A. Feldt, at the age of forty, returned to the Royal Australian Navy as a lieutenant-commander and was posted under the Director of Naval Intelligence as staff officer (intelligence) at Port Moresby. By December he had visited everyone who owned a teleradio in the Solomons, the New Hebrides, Papua, New Guinea, New Britain, New Ireland, and their "satellite specks of land". He issued instructions to all, and gave training to about a hundred others who might be able to report activities. They were island residents, planters, prospectors, missionaries, and government officials; in occupied jungle regions their reporting of movements classed them as spies, to be hunted down, tortured and killed. Only a few hundred men, all told, worked for Ferdinand, but they were the eyes and ears of the Allied forces throughout the Japanese advance and occupation, as well as the American counter-invasion and island-hopping campaigns. After the war, James A. Michener in *Tales of the South Pacific* (see No. 93) told of their heroic devotion, and Commander Feldt published the inside story of the coast watchers. "It is a story," he proclaims, "of damp, dimly lighted jungle camps, of hidden treetop lookouts; of silent submarines, landing a few intrepid men on hostile beaches, in the dead of night; of American airmen mysteriously rescued from enemy-held islands surrounded by enemy-dominated seas. It is the story of how Allied coast watchers managed, in strange and devious ways, not only to exist under the noses of the Japanese, but also to radio our vital military information. It is the story, too, of all the bravery, the loyalty, and the ingenuity of many tropical natives, and of the perfidy or weakness of others."

An addendum in the 1959 edition tells of the work of the coast watchers after September, 1944, when they broadened their scope to include the organization of native troops for guerrilla operations in the South Pacific. Previous to the end of hostilities, the casualties inflicted by the coast watchers and guerrillas were: enemy killed, 5,414; enemy wounded, 1,492; enemy captured, 74. Their own losses were: Europeans killed, 27; Europeans captured, 18 (only two survived); natives captured, 40; natives killed, 20. The section rescued 70 prisoners of war, 321 airmen, 280 naval personnel, 190 missionaries and civilians, and 260 Asians, as well as a large number of native refugees. The saving of Allied lives through their day-to-day observation and reporting of enemy activities cannot be calculated.

Commander Feldt, modest about his own leadership but eager to give factual accounts of the many exciting exploits of his men, had been one of the first cadets to enter the Royal Australian Naval College. He joined the Grand Fleet in European waters in 1917 as a midshipman and retired in 1922 with the rank of lieutenant. The following year he went to New Guinea in government service, and when another war came he was warden of the celebrated Wau goldfield. His naval service and his acquaintance with men in the islands made him the logical choice as organizer of the secret band whose existence was first known through his enduring book.

[93] JAMES A. MICHENER. *Tales of the South Pacific.* London and New York: Macmillan, 1947.

Proclaimed in the United States Senate later as "Mr. Pacific", James A. Michener was sent to that ocean as an officer in the United States Naval Reserve during World War II. As a trouble-shooter in aviation maintenance he was able to visit some fifty islands and observe the activities of civilians as well as members of various service branches. From his experience came his first and most widely known book.

Tales of the South Pacific, awarded the Pulitzer Prize for the best American novel of 1947, is on the whole the finest volume of fiction dealing with the war in the Pacific. It inspired Richard Rodgers and Oscar Hammerstein to write the musical comedy *South Pacific*, which ran for 1,925 performances on Broadway and was made into a memorable film.

Michener has published a dozen other books, most of them about other parts of the world than the Pacific. Several of them, however, aside from his giant novel *Hawaii*, do deal with this region. One of these is *Return to Paradise* (London: Secker & Warburg, 1952; New York: Random House, 1951), a volume by a former serviceman returning five years later to wartime scenes. Using a daring device, Michener wrote a series of factual essays about the various places visited, including Tahiti, Fiji, Guadalcanal, Espíritu Santo, and New Guinea. He then wrote a series of parallel short stories growing out of the themes of the essays. Thus the reader could see from each essay what Michener thought about the nine regions, and from the companion story could determine what each region thought about itself. Another book about the Pacific, in collaboration with A. Grove Day, is *Rascals in Paradise* (London: Secker & Warburg, 1957; New York: Random House, 1957), biographies of ten colorful characters who adventured in the Pacific over a period from 1595 to 1953. A bio-critical volume by A. Grove Day, reviewing Michener's work to 1963, is *James A. Michener* (New York: Twayne U.S. Authors Series No. 60, 1964).

[94] RICHARD TREGASKIS. *Guadalcanal Diary*. Redhill, Surrey: Wells Gardner, Darton, 1943. New York: Random House, 1943.

A crucial struggle in World War II in the Pacific was covered day by day by a correspondent with the front-line units of the first detachment of United States Marines.

Richard Tregaskis, a lanky newsman, began this diary on July 26, 1942, aboard a transport under secret orders. After the naval bombardment preceding the landing on Guadalcanal on August 7, the Marines climbed into barges and began their gruelling struggle with the Japanese. They captured the tiny, invaluable air strip built by the enemy, and hung on against innumerable attacks by superior air, land, and sea forces. In straightforward language, including interviews with many fighting men, the observer reports the heroism and danger that he shared along with the fighting men on that strategic island. (Tregaskis was especially exposed in the front line, since he is six feet, seven inches tall.) These were the Gethsemane weeks for the Americans, but help was on the way. On September 26, departing because his oversize shoes had worn out, Tregaskis flew in a B-17 bomber to embattled Bougainville Island on a roundabout way to Honolulu. The marines had opened a bloody campaign that eventually was to turn the tide for the American forces in the Pacific.

Tregaskis's first long work was chosen as a Book-of-the-Month. A revised softbound edition in 1959 was improved by the restoration of censor's cuts and by the inclusion of information of Japanese origin.

Author of a book that has long outlasted immediate interest, Richard Tregaskis was born in Elizabeth, New Jersey, in 1916. He was educated in private schools and won an A.B. degree from Harvard University in 1938. He had begun acting as a news reporter in college and continued in journalism. He was American Pacific Fleet correspondent in 1942 and 1943. Convalescing from a wound received in November, 1943, he covered the Mediterranean theater and then the European Western Front. After the war he continued to report from overseas and became as well a magazine and book writer. He has published some ten books, and has also written screen plays and documentaries, along with television programs. He is a fellow of the Royal Geographical Society and a member of the Academy of Motion Picture Arts and Sciences.

[95] EUGENE BURDICK. *The Blue of Capricorn.* London: Victor Gollancz, 1962. Boston: Houghton, Mifflin, 1961.

Among his other books and collaborations, Eugene Burdick (1919–1965) wrote one volume on the Pacific.

The Blue of Capricorn pays James A. Michener the compliment of imitation in using a structure which, like Michener's *Return to Paradise*, mingles short stories with factual essays. Five of the eighteen chapters are ostensibly fiction. Aside from several fine stories, the best chapters are those dealing with physical aspects of the great ocean, its surface, its depths, the sky above, and the differences between atolls and high islands. Least useful are his generalizations about Polynesians, Micronesians, and aborigines. The theme of the book seems mainly to show the conflict between the old ways of the bush and the new ways of the "beach".

Burdick was born in Iowa in 1918 but went as a child to California. He worked as a clerk, ditch digger, and truck driver in order to earn $150, enough to enable him to enter Stanford University. In 1941 he was graduated, married, and taken into the United States Navy. Sent to Guadalcanal, he began service for twenty-six months in the Pacific as a gunnery officer aboard various ships. Burdick returned to Stanford to take Wallace Stegner's writing course, and then won a Ph.D. at Oxford as a Rhodes scholar. While a professor of political science at the University of California he published his first novel. Thereafter he gained fame as co-author of *The Ugly American* (with William Lederer, London: Gollancz, 1959; New York: Norton, 1958) and *Fail-Safe* (with Harvey Wheeler, London: Hurst & Blackett, 1964; New York: McGraw-Hill, 1962). Burdick's fondness for the Pacific was shown by his custom of taking his family to spend part of each year on Mooréa, near Tahiti. Burdick died of a heart attack during a tennis match.

[96] IRA WOLFERT. *An Act of Love.* New York: Simon & Schuster, 1948; retold version, 1954.

One of the best novels about an American fighter in World War II in the Pacific is *An Act of Love*. The book also shows how an author, satisfied that he could improve on his original work, can turn his back on it and create a new version closer to his intentions.

The main character is Harry Brunner, a young Navy pilot who, after a transport is torpedoed in a terrifying sea battle, is washed up on a small, unnamed Pacific island. Nursed back to health by the native people, Brunner wins a girl named Tunumuza, who acquires from him an Occidental concept of love that separates her from the tribalism of her village. Brunner then joins the only white family on the island, and falls halfheartedly in love with the daughter, Julia; but his love is still inhibited by fear and self-distrust. When American forces invade the island, Brunner is able to help in the jungle fighting. His greatest battle, however, is within himself; and to resolve it requires an "act of love" that recognizes reality. Lieutenant Brunner is a man who has to "fight out to a peace the war between his boundlessness and its boundaries".

To take a published work and make of it something different and better requires not only an act of love but an act of great courage. Wolfert succeeds well in the retold version. It lacks the over-elaborate Freudian repetitions, and makes both combat and native village life more natural. As he says in a foreword to what is virtually a different novel, "the same characters (Brunner, and the Andersens, and Tunumuza and Sadokawa, and Youie Craik and Major Munday) are doing approximately the same things. But there are also new characters doing new things and the old characters also do new things. For in about half its length, this is an entirely new book and in the rest of it, it has been rewritten drastically."

Ira Wolfert was born in New York City in 1908 and attended public schools there. He worked his way through the Columbia School of Journalism as a streetcar motorman and as a taxi driver. Becoming a newspaper reporter in New York, he wrote dramatic criticism, sports, and general assignments. In 1942 and 1943 he traveled in the South Pacific as a war correspondent. He took part in a landing under fire on New Georgia in the Solomon Islands. As the war went on, a bullet creased his chest, and another chipped the bone under an eyebrow. He lay in a wet foxhole in the jungle for eight days and survived malaria, unable to reach a bed. Later he reported the Normandy landings, and was at St. Lo for the breakthrough, on the Seine with Patton, in Paris for the liberation, and in Germany for the storming of the Siegfried Line. His despatches from Solomons won him a Pulitzer Prize. Other books by Wolfert on the Pacific war include *Battle for the Solomons* (London: Jarrolds, 1943; Boston: Houghton, Mifflin, 1943); *Torpedo 8: the Story of Swede Larsen's Bomber Squadron* (London: Jarrolds, 1944; Boston: Houghton, Mifflin, 1943); and *American Guerrilla in the Philippines* (London: Gollancz, 1946; New York: Simon & Schuster, 1945), giving the true story of Lieutenant Iliff Richardson, who joined a Filipino band and helped to send out radio reports to General Douglas MacArthur until the islands were recaptured.

[97] PETER WORSLEY. *The Trumpet Shall Sound: A Study of "Cargo" Cults in Melanesia.* London: MacGibbon & Kee, 1957.

The last few decades in the South Pacific have witnessed various strange native religious movements. A prophet arises to announce the end of the world. After this cataclysm, the revered ancestors will return, or some other liberating power will appear, bringing all the goods the people desire. The believers prepare themselves for the millennium by setting up cults, building storehouses and docks to receive the expected goods or "cargo", and sometimes abandoning their gardens, eating all their food supplies and throwing away their money.

The meaning of such movements throughout the world in the past has been studied by anthropologists. Peter Worsley, who obtained his doctorate at the Australian National University, has here told of the various Melanesian cults in clear language and has summed up their connections with other "nativistic" rebellions.

Social change in our century has wrought wide unrest. *The Trumpet Shall Sound* tells of movements in Fiji, the Solomons, the New Hebrides, and a number of places in New Guinea. The marks of activist "millenarism" include: a group of disappointed peasants or dispossessed folk; resentment against a superior or foreign power; heresy; formation of idealistic cults with ranks, badges, and symbols; one or more prophets or "messiahs"; rites that appear to seek complete destruction of the existing order so that a new and higher order can suddenly be achieved: meetings that arouse hysteria and compulsive body movements such as the twitchings of the "Vailala madness"; defiance by youths of their elders; open flouting of sexual and other tabus in order to shatter all existing ties with outworn creeds; use of forbidden narcotics such as kava; meditation; and stress on personal moral renewal. Withdrawal to separate communities and building of storehouses to hold the expected "cargo" rewards that hitherto have been denied to the cultists are acts of faith channeling energy as well as demonstrating sincere belief.

Often the cults are triggered by the incursion of foreigners, such as the Japanese and Americans during World War II. As Worsley says, "The millenarian idea, then, is often introduced from the outside and injected into the movement. It then acts as a catalyst among people whose wants are rapidly developing, but who feel frustrated, deprived, and helpless. The tensions generated by the contradiction between the people's acceptance of what Merton calls 'cultural goals' and the lack of 'institutionalized means' through which to attain these goals result in a peculiarly explosive and emotionally-charged situation. The goals Merton discusses are those of American society, especially the achievement of monetary success. The goals of the Melanesian are different. They are conditioned by his notion of a *right* to the possession of the cargo, which the whites are perversely denying him. This right is not the same thing as the socialist's conception of rights in a product which is socially produced but privately appropriated. The Melanesian conception is conditioned by cultural and social values which include the idea of much wider rights in the property of others than we conceive of in our society. To exaggerate somewhat, deliberately, one might say that the product is privately produced but socially appropriated." In Melanesia, many of the cargo activities evolved into a growing nationalism that has today resulted in decolonization and slow success in self-government.

Dr. Worsley has made a complicated topic clear to the average reader who might be impatient with the jargon of sociology. He also abolishes some common fallacies. The "Marching Rule" movement of the Solomons, for instance, has been perverted into "Marxian Rule". It is true that some American servicemen during World War II may have given the natives a few crude ideas on Communism, but the term is actually drawn from Masinga Rule, using a word meaning "brotherhood". Later valuable studies are *Mambu: A Melanesian Millenium*, by Kenelm Burridge (London: Methuen, 1960) and *Road Belong Cargo*, by Peter Lawrence (Manchester: Manchester University Press, 1964).

[98] THOR HEYERDAHL. *The "Kon-Tiki" Expedition*. London: G. Allen & Unwin, 1952. *Kon-Tiki*. Chicago: Rand McNally & Co., 1950.

The book about the passage of a balsa raft in 1947 from Callao, Peru, to an atoll in the Tuamotu Archipelago, together with a 1951 film based on it, attracted popular imagination to the point where, to many people, the only volume on the South Pacific they can name is *Kon-Tiki*.

Five Norwegian men and one Swede (Bengt Danielsson—see No. 76), led by Thor Heyerdahl, formed the crew of a vessel of balsa wood, equipped with a sail and modern supplies, including a radio, plenty of food and water, and a rubber dinghy. The raft, towed off Callao, following favorable winds and currents floated 4,300 miles before crashing on a reef on the atoll of Raroia. The trip was uneventful except for plenty of good fishing; sharks and whales were seen, including a large whale shark. Excitement came when the raft crashed and the mast fell, although none of the crew was seriously hurt. The raft was salvaged and is now the center of interest in the Kon-Tiki Museum at Oslo, Norway. Heyerdahl's account of the adventure is decidedly a gripping story, and was hailed as an inspiration to those who admire daring and hardihood.

The sail of the raft bore the image of "Kon-Tiki", from the stone carving of a Peruvian sun-god who was supposed to have led a fair-skinned civilized people across the Pacific 1,500 years ago. As Heyerdal states in his appendix: "My migration theory, as such, was not necessarily proved by the successful outcome of the Kon-Tiki expedition. What we *did* prove was that the South

American balsa raft possesses qualities not previously known to scientists of our time, and that the Pacific islands are located well inside the range of prehistoric craft from Peru."

Stated briefly, Heyerdahl's theory claims that two different groups of American Indians populated the islands of Polynesia. First, a band of Peruvian Indians drifted out on rafts into the islands of eastern Polynesia, touching Easter Island and later moving westward through the Marquesas and the Society group to the western border of the Polynesian triangle. Second, a group of Indians from the Pacific Northwest paddled to Hawaii in dugout canoes, and then gradually filtered into the southern Polynesian islands, to mingle with the Peruvian strain already settled there. In his book, *American Indians in the Pacific* (London: G. Allen & Unwin, 1952), the theory is presumably supported by remarks on winds and currents, the origin of the sweet potato and blood-type distributions.

Prehistoric trans-Pacific voyages are quite conceivable, but little real information is available. Populating of the Philippine Islands by American Indians was proposed by a Spanish historian, Father Joaquín M. de Zúñiga, as early as 1803. Heyerdahl is the only outstanding ethnologist today, however, who assumes that the Polynesians originally were Amerinds. Dating of migrations is highly important. Dr. Robert C. Suggs, in Chapter 16, "The 'Kon-Tiki' Myth", of his *The Island Civilizations of Polynesia* (New York: New American Library, 1960), observes: "Heyerdahl's Peruvians must have availed themselves of that classical device of science fiction, the time machine, for they showed up off Easter Island in A.D. 380, led by a post-A.D. 750 Incan god-hero, with an A.D. 750 Tiahuanaco material culture featuring A.D. 1500 Incan walls, and not one thing characteristic of the Tiahuanaco period in Peru and Bolivia. This is equivalent to saying that America was discovered in the last days of the Roman Empire by King Henry the Eighth, who brought the Ford Falcon to the benighted aborigines" (224).

Heyerdahl was born in Norway in 1914 and did some graduate study at the University of Oslo and field work in Polynesia and British Columbia, "to test the theory that inhabitants of Pacific islands partly originated in prehistoric South America". After the *Kon-Tiki* book brought him funds, he led a Norwegian expedition to the Galápagos Islands in 1953 and a similar one to Easter Island in 1955–56, from which came the volume *Aku-Aku: The Secret of Easter Island* (London: G. Allen & Unwin, 1958; Chicago: Rand McNally & Co., 1958). *Sea Routes to Polynesia: American Indians and Early Asiastics in the Pacific* (London: G. Allen & Unwin, 1968; Chicago: Rand McNally & Co., 1968) is a collection of nine papers delivered before various bodies. Heyerdahl succeeded in 1970 in sailing an Egyptian reed boat across the Atlantic to demonstrate the possibility of Egyptian-American contact. He has received various honors and is a member of a number of societies.

Readers interested in rafting in the Pacific might also enjoy several other books. Among these is *The Voyage of the "Kaimiloa"* by Eric de Bisschop, translated from the French by Marc Ceppi (London: G. Bell, 1940), describing how the author and Jacques Tatibouet sailed from Hawaii to Marseilles in southern France during World War II in a homemade craft. De Bisschop's other book, *Tahiti-Nui*, translated from the French by Edward Young (New York: McDowell, Oblensky, 1959), tells of his attempt to reverse the *Kon-Tiki* theory by sailing a bamboo raft from Tahiti to South America. Bengt Danielsson's *From Raft to Raft* (see No. 76) tells of De Bisschop's voyage and his death on a return journey. Another man who finally lost his life rafting in the Pacific was the elderly William Willis. His first book is *The Epic Voyage of the "Seven Little Sisters"* (London: Hutchinson, 1956; *The Gods Were Kind*, New York: E. P. Dutton, 1955), describing how, with only a parrot and a cat for company, Willis floated from Callao to Pago Pago in Samoa, exceeding the distance of the *Kon-Tiki* by 4,300 miles. Willis's last book, describing his voyage on the raft *Age Unlimited*, is *An Angel on Each Shoulder* (London: Hutchinson, 1966; *Whom the Sea Hath Taken*, New York: Meredith Press, 1966). DeVere Baker's book, *The Raft "Lehi IV"* (Long Beach, California: Whitehorn Publishing Co., 1959) tells how, to demonstrate a Mormon theory, Baker and his crew floated for sixty-nine days between Californian and Hawaiian waters. *The Raft*, by Robert Trumbull (New York: Henry Holt, 1942) is a classic of survival by three downed American Navy flyers in World War II.

[99] LEO DANIEL BRONGERSMA and G. F. VENEMA. *To the Mountains of the Stars.* Translated from the Dutch by Alan G. Readett. Garden City, New York: Doubleday, 1963.

The best account of the seldom explored Stone Age regions of what was still central Dutch New Guinea is given in this record of an air-supported expedition in 1959. The members charted jungle areas, meandering rivers, and treetop villages on their pioneer journey from the southern lowlands through the mountains to Hollandia on the northern coast.

Most of the writing, compiled from many notes by members of the expedition, is by Brongersma, a scientist well known in the Netherlands, supplemented by the contributions of Flight-Lieutenant Venema, in charge of the air service, which included helicopters. The maps and photographs are excellent.

[100] JAMES RAMSEY ULLMAN. *Where the Bong Tree Grows: the Log of One Man's Journey in the South Pacific.* Cleveland, Ohio: World, 1963.

Ullman, born in New York in 1907 and educated at Princeton, novelist and traveler, escaped to the Pacific in the early 1960s to seek balm for personal and professional wounds. He made a "counterclockwise" tour, in various types of vessel, of Micronesia, Fiji, Tonga, Samoa, Tahiti, and the Cook group, and returned to the United States on a yacht via the Marquesas. A skilled observer and writer, Ullman nevertheless is hampered by the ghosts of all the authors who preceded him in the region. Pages are filled with South Sea gossip and clichés, and the writing reveals the weariness of a tired author who is flogging himself through "paradise". More successful is *Island Below the Wind* (London: Collins, 1962); *Fia Fia* (New York: World, 1962), a novel set in an imaginary group of islands that obviously resembles American Samoa.

APPENDIX

SOME ADDITIONAL REFERENCES ON THE PACIFIC ISLANDS

APPENDIX

SOME ADDITIONAL REFERENCES ON THE PACIFIC ISLANDS

AINSLIE, KENNETH. *Pacific Ordeal.* New York: Norton, 1956. The dangerous peacetime voyage of a seagoing tug from Panama across the Pacific, narrated by the captain of a motley crew.

ANDERSON, CHARLES ROBERTS. *Melville in the South Seas.* New York: Columbia University Press, 1939. A comprehensive study, not greatly corrected by later scholars.

BAIN, KENNETH. *The Friendly Islanders: the Story of Queen Salote and Her People.* London: Hodder & Stoughton, 1967. A popular history of Tonga.

BARNARD, Charles H. *Narrative of the Sufferings and Adventures of Capt. Charles H. Barnard in a Voyage Round the World . . .* New York: printed for the author by J. Lindon, 1829. Travels of an American seafarer from 1812 to 1816.

BARRETT, CHARLES LESLIE (ed.). *The Pacific: Ocean of Islands.* Melbourne: N. H. Seward, 1950. A miscellaneous collection of essays.

BARRETT, CHARLES LESLIE. *White Blackfellows: The Strange Adventures of Europeans Who Lived Among Savages.* Melbourne: Hallcraft, 1948. Interesting collection about men who "went native".

BEAGLEHOLE, J. C. *The Exploration of the Pacific.* London: A. & C. Black, 1934; New York: Macmillan, 1934. 3rd ed., reset, London: A. & C. Black, 1966; Stanford, Calif.: Stanford University Press, 1966. A standard account up to 1780.

BEECHEY, FREDERICK WILLIAM. *Narrative of a Voyage to the Pacific and Beering's Strait . . . in H.M.S. "Blossom", 1825–1828.* 2 vol. London: H. Colburn & R. Bentley, 1831. A scientific expedition that still sought a "northwest passage" in the Arctic.

BENNETT, FREDERICK DEBELL. *Narrative of a Whaling Voyage Around the Globe, 1835 to 1836.* 2 vol. London: R. Bentley, 1840. An important volume on whaling previous to Melville's *Moby Dick.*

BORDEN, CHARLES. *South Sea Islands.* Philadelphia: Macrae Smith, 1961. A readable account of the main island peoples, especially in recent years.

Bougainville, Louis Antoine de. *A Voyage Round the World . . . in the Years 1766–69*. Translated from the French by John Reinhold Forster. London: Nourse, 1772. This was the first French circumnavigation. The two ships independently discovered Tahiti.

Bryan, Edwin H., Jr. *American Polynesia and the Hawaiian Chain*. rev. ed. Honolulu: Tongg, 1942. Much information, still valid, on the many Pacific islands under the American flag.

Buck, Sir Peter H. *Ethnology of Mangareva*. Honolulu: Bishop Museum Bulletin No. 157, 1938. Contains many songs and chants.

Buck, Peter H. *Explorers of the Pacific*. Honolulu: Bishop Museum Special Publication No. 43, 1953. Abstracts of voyages and good bibliographies.

Bühler, Alfred, Terry Barrow, and Charles P. Mountford. *Oceania and Australia: The Art of the South Sea Islands*. London: Methuen, 1962; New York: Crown, n.d. Historical, sociological, and religious backgrounds of art, with many illustrations.

Burney, James. *A Chronological History of the Discoveries in the South Sea or Pacific Ocean*. 5 vol. London: L. Hansard, 1803–1817. One of Cook's officers, who became an admiral, wrote five volumes covering earliest voyages by Europeans and reached no further than 1764.

Burns, Sir Alan Cuthbert. *Fiji*. London: H.M. Stationery Office, 1963. An excellent recent history.

Calkin, Milo. *The Last Voyage of the "Independence"*. San Francisco: Weiss Printing Co., 1953. After trading among the islands, the ship was wrecked on Starbuck in the Line group; survivors made an open-boat passage of fifteen hundred miles to one of the Hervey Islands and thence to Rarotonga.

Calkins, Fay. *My Samoan Chief*. New York: Doubleday, 1962. An American girl married a Samoan and for a time lived with his family and managed a plantation in American Samoa.

Cary, William S. *Wrecked on the Feejees . . .* Nantucket, Mass.: Inquirer and Mirror Press, 1928. Cary was sole survivor of the massacre of the whaler *Oeno* in 1825 and, adopted by the "king" of Turtle Island, lived for nine years among cannibals.

Cheever, Rev. Henry T. *The Island World of the Pacific . . .* Glasgow: W. Collins, 1850?; New York: Harper, 1850. Missionary endeavor in Hawaii and other parts of Polynesia.

Churchward, William Brown. *Blackbirding in the South Pacific*. London: Swan Sonnenschein, 1888. A South Sea consul tells of labor recruiting methods.

CHURCHWARD, WILLIAM BROWN. *My Consulate in Samoa*. London: R. Bentley, 1887. Amusing stories by a young Englishman who spent four years in the troubled islands.

COFFIN, ROBERT. *The Last of the "Logan"* . . . ed. Harold W. Thompson. Ithaca, N.Y.: Cornell University Press, 1941. A whaler between 1854 and 1859, Coffin was wrecked and lived among the Fijians.

COLLOCOTT, E. E. V. *Tales and Poems of Tonga*. Honolulu: Bishop Museum Bulletin No. 46, 1928. A welcome addition to Tongan native literature.

COLNETT, JAMES. *A Voyage to the South Atlantic and Around Cape Horn into the Pacific Ocean . . . in the Ship "Rattler"*. London: printed for the author by W. Bennett, 1798. Colnett, who voyaged widely in the Pacific, opened the whaling grounds in that ocean.

COOPER, H. STONEHEWER. *The Islands of the Pacific*. London: R. Bentley, 1888. A two-volume revision of his *Coral Lands*, London: R. Bentley, 1880. Both books contain many useful facts.

CORNEY, B. GLANVILL (ed.). *The Quest and Occupation of Tahiti, by Emissaries of Spain During 1772–1776* . . . London: Hakluyt Society, Second Series, XXXII (1913), XXXVI (1915), and XLIII (1918). Compiled and translated by the editor. Describe the two Spanish attempts to convert the Tahitians between Cook's voyages.

COULTER, JOHN. *Adventures in the Pacific* . . . Dublin: W. Curry; London, Longmans, Brown, 1845. An English M.D. voyaged to the Pacific in the *North America*.

COULTER, JOHN. *Adventures on the Western Coast of South America* . . . 2 vol. London: Longman, Brown, Green & Longmans, 1847. A sequel covering incidents in the Gilberts, New Ireland, New Britain, New Guinea, and other islands.

COWAN, JAMES. *Suwarrow Gold and Other Stories of the Great South Sea*. London: Cape, 1936. Tales by a New Zealand historian and collector of folklore who spent some time on Suvorov Island.

COX, EDWARD GODFREY. *A Reference Guide to the Literature of Travel* 3 vol. Seattle, Wash.: University of Washington Press, 1935—. An annotated bibliography; in Vol. I, "Circumnavigations", and Vol. II, "South Seas", all books on subjects to 1800 printed in Great Britain are given chronologically.

DERRICK, R. A. *A History of Fiji*. Vol. I. Suva: Government Printer. A good pioneer account; the later volume was never published.

DICKINSON, J. H. C. *A Trader in the Savage Solomons*. London: H. F. & G. Witherby, 1927. One of the best accounts of trading in the Solomons during the present century.

"DIVINE, DAVID" [ARTHUR DURHAM DIVINE]. *The King of Fassari.* London: Murray, 1951; New York: Macmillan, 1950. American military men meet Pacific islanders in World War II and after.

DUNBABIN, THOMAS. *Slavers of the South Seas.* Sydney: Angus & Robertson, 1935. Authentic stories of kidnapping natives for labor on plantations.

DUNMORE, JOHN. *French Explorers in the Pacific.* Vol. I: The Eighteenth Century. London: Oxford University Press, 1965. A scholarly work planned to give a panorama of French exploration from the closing years of the eighteenth century to the middle of the nineteenth.

ELBERT, SAMUEL H. "Chants and Love Songs of the Marquesas Islands, French Oceania", *Journal of the Polynesian Society*, L, 1941. Literal translations of symbol-laden Polynesian poetry.

FINDLAY, ALEXANDER GEORGE. *A Directory for the Navigation of the South Pacific Ocean* . . . 4th ed. London: R. H. Laurie, 1877. Outdated for navigation, but filled with early reports on islands and passages and reports of sightings.

FISHER, JOHN. *The Midmost Waters: Biography of an Ocean.* London: Naldrett Press, 1952. Essays on Pacific writers and other travelers.

FREEMAN, OTIS W. (ed.). *Geography of the Pacific.* London: Chapman & Hall, 1951; New York: Wiley, 1951. A collection of essays by various authorities, still valuable on many points but in need of revision.

FRIIS, HERMAN (ed.). *The Pacific Basin: A History of Its Geographical Exploration.* New York: American Geographical Society, 1967. Scholarly papers derving from a symposium at the Tenth Pacific Science Congress, 1961, with a lengthy bibliography.

GERBAULT, ALAIN. *The Gospel of the Sun.* London: Hodder & Stoughton, 1933. *In Quest of the Sun: the Journal of the "Firecrest".* New York: Doubleday, Doran, 1930. A French adventurer took six years to sail around the world in an eight-ton yacht, and was buried among the islands.

GRATTAN, C. HARTLEY. *The Southwest Pacific to 1900.* Ann Arbor, Mich.: University of Michigan Press, 1963. As well as the Pacific Islands, this history includes Australia and Antarctica.

GRATTAN, C. HARTLEY. *The Southwest Pacific Since 1900.* Same.

Great Britain: Hydrographic Office, Admiralty. *Pacific Islands Pilot.* 3 vol. 8th ed., 1956–57, with supplements. Sailing directions, maps, and bibliographies.

Great Britain: Naval Intelligence Division. *Pacific Islands.* 4 vol. Geographical Handbook Series, 1939–1945. Vol. I has a hundred-page brief history of the Pacific and a bibliography up to World War II.

GUIART, JEAN. *The Arts of the South Pacific*. Translated from the French by Anthony Christie. London: Thames & Hudson, 1963; New York: Golden Press, 1963. A magnificent treatment, with more than 400 illustrations.

HARRISSON, THOMAS H. *Savage Civilisation*. London: Gollancz, 1937. Story of a young man taken into a tribe of the fierce people of the interior of Malekula in Melanesia.

HAUGLAND, VERN. *Letter from New Guinea*. London: Hammond, 1944; New York: Farrar & Rinehart, 1943. An American flyer in World War II was forced down and spent days escaping through jungle and over ridges.

HENDERSON, GEORGE C. *The Discoverers of the Fiji Islands*. London: J. Murray, 1933. Essays on Tasman, Cook, Bligh, James Wilson, and Bellingshausen.

HIGHLAND, GENEVIEVE A. *et al.* (eds.). *Polynesian Cultural History: Essays in Honor of Kenneth P. Emory*. Honolulu: Bishop Museum Special Publication No. 56, 1967. Excellent papers and bibliographies.

HOLDEN, HORACE. *A Narrative of the Shipwreck, Captivity, and Sufferings of Horace Holden and Benj. H. Nute . . .* Boston: Russell, Shattuck, 1836. Holden, with the rest of the crew of the *Mentor*, was wrecked in the Palau group in Micronesia in 1832; his account of two years spent among the people is harrowing but instructive.

HOLMES, WILFRED J. *Undersea Victory: The Influence of Submarine Operations on the War in the Pacific*. New York: Doubleday, 1966. Definitive volume on submarine achievements in World War II.

HORT, DORA. *Tahiti: Garden of the Pacific*. London: T. Fisher Unwin, 1891. Life in French Oceania during the 1880s is shown in this informal account, which includes descriptions of customs among both Tahitians and the foreign colony.

IRELAND, JOHN. *The Shipwrecked Orphans . . .* New Haven, Conn.: S. Babcock, 1845 (ed. "Thomas Teller"). A very rare little book about John Ireland and a child who were wrecked on the *Charles Eaton* and lived among the Murray Islanders of Torres Strait.

JOHNSON, IRVING. *Westward Bound in the Schooner "Yankee"*. New York: Norton, 1936. Among the best of the yachting chronicles; the *Yankee* hull is still visible on the reef at Rarotonga.

JONES, JOHN D. *Life and Adventure in the South Pacific*, by A Roving Printer. New York: Harper, 1861. Account of a whaling voyage from New Bedford around the Pacific, by "two young men" who spent five years in the fisheries; many islands were visited and shipboard life is amusingly described.

Journal of Pacific History. New York: Oxford University Press, 1966—. An annual volume of scholarly articles and reviews; extremely valuable for any student.

Journal of the Polynesian Society. Wellington: 1892—. An established scholarly quarterly of high value in Pacific studies. The Society also issues Memoirs and other publications.

KEESING, FELIX M. *The South Seas in the Modern World*. New York: John Day, 1941; rev. ed. 1945. Still useful for descriptions by a sociologist of the 1940s.

KEMP, PETER K. and LLOYD, CHRISTOPHER. *Brethren of the Coast: Buccaneers of the South Seas*. London: Heinemann, 1960; New York: St. Martin's Press, 1961. Good chapters on the Caribbean as well as on the Pacific region.

LAMBERT, SYLVESTER M. *A Yankee Doctor in Paradise*. Boston: Little, Brown, 1941. Problems of native health and customs, revealed by an M.D. in the Pacific Islands.

LANGSDORFF, GEORG H. VON. *Voyages and Travels in Various Parts of the World . . . 1803–1807*. 2 vol. London: H. Colburn, 1813–14. An observer on the Russian survey ships *Nadeshda* and *Neva*.

LLOYD, CHRISTOPHER. *Pacific Horizons: The Exploration of the Pacific before Capt. Cook*. London: Allan & Unwin, 1946; New York: Macmillan, 1947. A sound and readable account up to 1780.

LOCKERBY, WILLIAM. *The Journal of William Lockerby*, ed. Sir Everard im Thurn and Leonard C. Wharton. London: Hakluyt Society, Second Series, LII, 1925. Lockerby, a sandalwood hunter, was a castaway in Fiji in 1808 and became a chief.

LUBBOCK, BASIL. *Bully Hayes*. Boston: Lauriat, 1931. Highly fictionized; legend rather than biography.

LUKE, SIR HARRY. *Islands of the South Pacific*. London: Harrap, 1962. Well-told accounts of various groups, with some good pictures, by a former governor of Fiji and high commissioner for the Western Pacific.

MALINOWSKY, BRONISLAW. *Argonauts of the Western Pacific*. London: Routledge, 1922; New York: Dutton, 1922. A lengthy study of native sailing and trading in the archipelagoes of New Guinea, by a noted anthropologist.

MARKHAM, ALBERT H. *The Cruise of the "Rosario" Amongst the New Hebrides and Santa Cruz Islands* . . . London: Sampson Low, Marston, Low & Searle, 1873. A British naval commander exposes evils of Melanesian blackbirding.

MASON, HENRIETTA. *White Orchid.* New York: Longmans, 1953. A New Zealand girl's life as a governess in the New Hebrides in our century.

MAUDE, H. E. *Of Islands and Men: Studies in Pacific History.* Melbourne: Oxford University Press, 1968. Excellent essays, especially on the *Bounty* mutineers, Spanish and post-Spanish discoveries, beachcombers and castaways, and trading in the Pacific.

MÉTRAUX, A. *Easter Island: A Stone Age Civilization of the Pacific.* New York: Oxford University Press, 1957. The best single book of a number on the "mystery" of Easter; it contains a sketch of the history of the island since European contact.

Mitchell Library, the Public Library of New South Wales. *Dictionary Catalogue of Printed Books.* 38 vol. Boston: G. K. Hall, 1968. A treasury of titles on the Pacific region.

MOOREHEAD, ALAN. *The Fatal Impact: an Account of the Invasion of the South Pacific, 1767–1840.* New York: Harper & Row, 1966. Sections on Tahiti, Australia, and Antarctica; the Tahiti section is based heavily on Beaglehole's books.

MORRELL, BENJAMIN, JR. *A Narrative of Four Voyages to the South Seas . . . from the Year 1822 to 1831.* New York: Harper, 1832. Travel accounts by an American sea captain.

MOSS, FREDERICK J. *Through Atolls and Islands in the Great South Sea.* London: Sampson Low, Marston, Serle & Rivington, 1889. Good descriptions by a New Zealander, a planter and trader; based mainly on a voyage in 1886.

MUSPRATT, ERIC. *My South Sea Island.* London: Hopkinson, 1931. Amusing report of the stay of a wanderer on San Cristóbal in the Solomons.

MYTINGER, CAROLINE. *Headhunting in the Solomon Islands Around the Coral Sea.* London: Macmillan, 1943; New York: Macmillan, 1942. The author and her companion, Margaret Warner, traveled through Melanesia before World War II, recording their adventures while obtaining "heads" and other paintings of the native people and resident Europeans.

NEWBURY, COLIN W. (ed.). *The History of the Tahitian Mission, 1799–1830.* London: Hakluyt Society, Second Series, CXVI, 1961. This history by John Davies is essential to an understanding of the London Missionary Society's work.

NOZIKOV, NIKOLAI N. *Russian Voyages Round the World,* ed. and with an introduction by M. A. Sergeyev. Translated from the Russian by Ernst and Mira Lesser. London: Hutchinson, n.d. Recounts voyages of I. F. Krusenstern and Y. F. Lisyansky, V. M. Golovnin, and F. P. Litke.

Oceania. Melbourne: Macmillan, 1930—. A journal devoted to the study of the native peoples of Australia, New Guinea, and the Pacific Islands.

OLIVER, DOUGLAS. *The Pacific Islands.* Cambridge, Mass.: Harvard University Press, 1951. A softbound revision (New York: Doubleday, 1961) of this standard work contains an extended bibliography.

OLIVER, JAMES. *The Wreck of the "Glide".* Boston: W. D. Ticknor, 1846. An account of life and manners in the Fiji group; the second edition (London and New York: Wiley & Putnam, 1848) has additional chapters written or edited by William Giles Dix.

Pacific Islands Monthly. Sydney: Pacific Publications, 1930—. Historical accounts as well as news of interest to residents are found in this illustrated magazine.

PALMER, GEORGE. *Kidnapping in the South Sea . . .* Edinburgh: Edmonson & Douglas, 1871. A narrative of a three-month cruise by the captain of H.M.S. *Rosario.*

PATTERSON, SAMUEL. *Narrative of the Adventures and Sufferings of Samuel Patterson . . .* Providence, Mass.: Palmer, 1817. An American seaman shipwrecked in 1808 on one of the Fiji group lived for six months as a commoner among the Melanesians.

PELLATON, MAY [LARSEN] and HARRY LARSEN. *The Golden Cowrie: New Caledonia.* Translated from the French by James Hogarth. Edinburgh: Oliver & Boyd, 1961. A good account of this big island in Melanesia.

POIGNANT, ROSLYN. *Oceanic Mythology.* London: Hamlyn, 1967. A popular account with many illustrations.

PRICE, SIR A. GRENFELL. *The Western Invasions of the Pacific and Its Continents.* London: Oxford University Press, 1963. A rounded study of the reciprocal influences of Europeans and native peoples of the Pacific Basin.

PRIDAY, H. E. L. *Cannibal Island: The Turbulent Story of New Caledonia's Cannibal Coasts.* Wellington: Reed, 1944. An interesting account by a traveler and South Sea trader.

PRITCHARD, WILLIAM THOMAS. *Polynesian Reminiscences, or Life in the South Pacific Islands.* London: Chapman & Hall, 1866. Pritchard is an excellent source on Samoa and Fiji.

QUAIN, BUELL H. *The Flight of the Chiefs: Epic Poetry of Fiji.* New York: J. J. Augustin, 1942. Translations by a skilled anthropologist.

RAMSDEN, ERIC. *Strange Stories from the South Seas.* Wellington: Reed, 1944. Yarns of seafaring.

REEVES, EDWARD. *Brown Men and Women; or The South Sea Islands in 1895 and 1896.* London: Swan Sonnenschein, 1898. Chatty yarns of Tonga, Samoa, Fiji, Cook Islands, and Society group, with sixty photographs, some obviously "posed".

REYNOLDS, JEREMIAH N. *Voyage of the United States Frigate "Potomac".* New York: Harper, 1835. Account of the circumnavigation made between 1831 and 1834 under Commodore John Downes.

RIESENBERG, FELIX. *The Pacific Ocean.* London and New York: McGraw-Hill, 1940. Somewhat dated but still interesting.

ROBERTSON, REV. H. A. *Erromanga, the Martyr Isle.* Edited by John Fraser. London: Hodder & Stoughton, 1902. An account of history and customs, based on thirty years of missionary activity on an island in the New Hebrides.

ROGERS, STANLEY. *The Pacific.* London: Harrap, 1931. Sea yarns, illustrated by the author.

ROSENDAL, JORGEN. *The Happy Lagoons; the World of Queen Salote.* London: Jarrolds, 1961. Descriptions of latter-day Tonga.

ROWE, NEWTON A. *Samoa Under the Sailing Gods.* London and New York: Putnam, 1930. Missionary activities in the Samoan group.

RUHEN, OLAF. *Minerva Reef.* London: Angus & Robertson, 1963. The future of a Tongan crew of seventeen seemed hopeless when their cutter was wrecked in 1962, but they survived for 102 days before rescue came through the cruise of a small decked vessel built on the reef and sailed to Kandavu in Fiji.

SHADBOLT, MAURICE and RUHEN, OLAF. *Isles of the South Pacific.* Washington: National Geographic Society, 1968. Some descriptions and excellent color photographs.

SHARP, ANDREW. *The Discovery of the Pacific Islands.* London: Oxford University Press, 1960, 1962, 1969. A monumental study of first sightings, still capable of correction.

SHINEBERG, DOROTHY. *They Came for Sandalwood: A Study of the Sandalwood Trade in the South-West Pacific, 1830–1865.* Melbourne: Melbourne University Press, 1967; London and New York: Cambridge University Press, 1967. A factual and interesting account of this early trade.

SIMPSON, COLIN. *Islands of Men: Inside Melanesia.* Sydney: Angus & Robertson, 1955. Stories and good pictures by an Australian travel writer.

SKELTON, R. A. *Explorers' Maps.* New York: Praeger, 1958. Part V deals with "The South Sea".

SLADE, JOHN. *Old Slade; or, Fifteen Years Adventures of a Sailor . . .* ed. Charles W. Denison. Boston: J. Putnam, 1844. These reminiscences include a residence among cannibals on the Wallis Islands.

SMITH, BERNARD. *European Vision and the South Pacific, 1768–1850: A Study in the History of Art and Ideas*. London: Oxford University Press, 1960. An excellent study of the slow achievement of Pacific artists in representing the South Seas through their own eyes.

SPOEHR, FLORENCE MANN. *White Falcon*. Palo Alto, Calif.: Pacific Books, 1963. Essays on the Hamburg trading empire of Godeffroy.

STACKPOLE, EDOUARD. *The Sea-Hunters: The New England Whalemen During Two Centuries, 1635–1835*. Philadelphia: Lippincott, 1953. An exciting chronicle of American whaling, especially in the Pacific.

STIMSON, J. FRANK. *Tuamotuan Legends*. Honolulu: Bishop Museum Bulletin No. 148, 1937. Collection by a resident of Tahiti.

STRAUSS, W. PATRICK. *Americans in Polynesia, 1783–1842*. East Lansing, Mich.: Michigan State University Press, 1963. A well-researched account, covering early visitors, traders, whalers, missionaries, naval officers, government agents, the United States Exploring Expedition, and American authors in Polynesia.

SUGGS, ROBERT C. *The Island Civilizations of Polynesia*. New York: New American Library, 1960. Descriptions of the regions by an American anthropologist.

TETENS, ALFRED. *Among the Savages of the South Seas*. Translated from the German by Florence Mann Spoehr. Stanford, Calif.: Stanford University Press, 1958. A naturalist in Palau and Yap.

TRUMBULL, ROBERT. *Paradise in Trust: A Report on Americans in Micronesia, 1946–1958*. New York: Sloane, 1959. Highly readable but already dated account of progress in the Trust Territory of the Pacific.

TUDOR, JUDY. *Many a Green Isle*. Sydney: Pacific Publications, 1966. Travels of an editor of *Pacific Islands Monthly*.

TUDOR, JUDY (ed.). *Pacific Islands Year Book and Who's Who*. 10th ed. Sydney: Pacific Publications, 1968. The best handbook available; packed with facts and maps.

VAYDA, ANDREW P. (ed.). *Peoples and Cultures of the Pacific*. New York: Doubleday, for American Museum of Natural History, 1968. A lengthy, up-to-date anthropological reader by various authorities.

WAGNER, HENRY R. *Sir Francis Drake's Voyage Round the World: Its Aims and Achievements*. San Francisco: John Howell, 1926. A large, documented volume with good illustrations and maps.

WALLIS, MARY DAVIS COOK. *Life in Feejee: or Five Years among the Cannibals*. Boston: W. Heath, 1851. Wife of the captain of the Salem trading vessel *Zotoff*, Mrs. Wallis accompanied her husband on two voyages and gives almost incredible accounts of true adventures among the cannibals.

WHEELER, DANIEL. *Memoirs of the Life and Gospel Labors of the Late Daniel Wheeler*. London: Harvey & Darton, 1842. A Quaker missionary who was used as a source by Melville.

WINGERT, PAUL S. *Art of the South Pacific Islands*. London: Thames & Hudson, 1953; New York: Beechhurst Press, n.d. A well-illustrated description.

WISE, HENRY A. *Los Gringos: or an Inside View of . . . Polynesia*. London: R. Bentley, 1849; New York: Baker & Scribner, 1849. A lieutenant in the American Navy voyaged among the islands in 1848.

WROTH, LAWRENCE C. *The Early Cartography of the Pacific*. New York: Papers of the Bibliographical Society of America, XXXVIII, 1944. An authoritative essay, with twenty-two maps.

INDEX OF PACIFIC NAMES AND PLACES